Boy from Kahaluu

Boy from Kahaluu

AN AUTOBIOGRAPHY

By

Tom Ige

Published by
Kin Cho Jin Kai
Honolulu

Library of Congress Cataloging-in-Publication Data

Ige, Tom, 1916–
    Boy from Kahaluu : an autobiography / by Tom Ige.
      p.   cm.
    ISBN 0-8248-1291-3
    1. Ige, Tom, 1916–   . 2. Economists—United States—Biography.
I. Title.
HB119.I34   1989
330'.092—dc20
[B]   89-19761
                                                                 CIP

∞™ The paper used in this publication meets the minimum requirements of
American National Standard for Information Sciences—Permanence of paper
for Printed Library Materials
                                              ANSI Z39.48–1984

Distributed by
University of Hawaii Press
Order Department
2840 Kolowalu Street
Honolulu, Hawaii 96822

Dedicated to Kyuzo Toyama
Father of Okinawan Immigration

*"Come, let's go
Our home will be
The five continents"*
Toyama, 1900

Contents

Foreword

Dr. Tom Ige has written a compelling account of his life, which captures the essence of the immigrant experience in Hawaii, from the hardship of growing up in his native and then-remote Kahaluu to the crisis of World War II and postwar success as a respected and traveled professional.

Ige's book, published in connection with the 90th anniversary of Okinawan immigration to Hawaii, is a roll call of famous Hawaii names from sports, politics, and academia, enlivened throughout with personal anecdotes that provide a poignant touch to many of his memories.

He recounts for us the isolation of a small agricultural community; the importance of baseball to the emerging Nisei generation; the pain of questioned loyalty during World War II; the bitterness of combat on his ancestral island; and the ultimate triumph of the children of Hawaii's immigrants in the postwar period.

Ige has heroes aplenty and fascinating experiences to match. His life has been a saga of involvement in the evolution of modern Hawaiian society.

Here, too, are his connections with contemporary political figures and the issues of the postwar decades. He does not seek to assess blame, offering instead his personal experiences and the flavor of the times.

In this work Dr. Ige takes us, as he says, on a journey. It is at once personal and immediate, distinguished by the width of his acquaintance and the breadth of his experience. It is a story for all who care about the islands and their people.

JOHN WAIHEE
Governor
State of Hawaii

A Prefatory Note

Written in a relaxed, "talk-story," matter-of-fact manner, Professor Ige has documented a valuable piece of Hawaiiana in its broadest sense. This book is a representation not only of Tom Ige's life but of the lives of nearly all of the Nisei who are his contemporaries.

In my personal view, which is reinforced as the years go by, the Nisei as members of a Hawaii sub-culture can be broadly categorized as having traversed one or a combination of three major routes in their journey through life. Practically all share the common experience of growing up in a rural plantation community or in an urban setting, in a bilingual—albeit pidgin English and pidgin Japanese—family, attending public schools, and graduating from high schools in Hawaii.

One category of Nisei traveled through the route shared by all and settled into vocations after high school or continued on to higher education and settled into businesses or professions without serving in the military.

The second category of Nisei saw their lives interrupted drastically by volunteering or being drafted into military service, literally ending their lives or returning to go on to higher education or settling into the work force.

The third category, the so-called Kibei, left Hawaii, usually after graduation from high school or intermediate school, for further study in Japan to return and settle into the work force or continue their education in colleges or universities.

Some traveled on all three routes and more as they grew and matured. By "more" I mean the experience of living a substantial time on the mainland for education or work; the significantly continuous participation in organized sports in which the Nisei was a major force; the attainment of the highest educational level, the doctorate; and participation in the political revolution which transformed Hawaii into the modern state of today. Tom Ige represents this unique group of Nisei as can be clearly discerned in this book.

By humbly yet candidly describing his life, Tom Ige touches the sensibility of all Nisei no matter which route he or she has traversed. While not truly a Kibei in the generic sense of the term, Tom tasted formal education in Okinawa as a child; he shared the public school experience of all Nisei; he served in the military well, even being severely wounded; he participated in baseball as a star player; he went on into higher education attaining a doctorate; while never holding elective office, he was at the core of all significant political activities of the revolutionary times in Hawaii's transition from territorial status to statehood; he traveled to foreign lands on invitation to advise foreign governments; and he distinguished himself as a professor at the University of Hawaii as well as at other mainland universities.

Tom Ige, by documenting his life, has demonstrated his faithfulness to his roots. By so doing, he reminds all, particularly the Nisei, of the richness of one's life we often take for granted. By leaving for posterity the route he had traversed and the happy times and painful moments therein, he adds yet another significant page to the contributions the Nisei have made to the United States of America.

ALBERT H. MIYASATO
former United Japanese Society President 1978–1980
former Deputy Superintendent of Schools
State of Hawaii

Acknowledgments

Many individuals have been of great assistance to me in bringing this book to fruition. Dr. Albert Miyasato, in particular, offered valuable advice and encouragement throughout the undertaking. The manuscript was read in its entirety by Dr. Franklin Oda, Director of the University of Hawaii Ethnic Studies Program, Dr. Seymour Ludsky, former head of the American Studies Program, and Dr. Shinye Gima of the University of Hawaii College of Education and wartime companion. Their evaluations and criticisms have been most helpful.

Governor John Waihee has been most gracious in providing the Foreword. Since his wife provided active leadership in the establishment of the Bunka-Kai-Kan, the Okinawan Cultural Center in Hawaii, I hope this book will add to the perpetuation of our heritage.

Tom Coffman, a long time observer of the political scene in Hawaii, has been most kind in permitting me to quote extensively from his excellent book, *Catch a Wave.* Although I was technically the campaign manager for Tom Gill in the 1970 Governor's race, I was immobilized with tuberculosis during this crucial period. I thankfully accept Coffman's account of this campaign.

I am also indebted to Masahide Ota whose book, *The Battle of Okinawa,* provided very useful information on the American invasion of Kerama during the early phase of the Okinawan campaign and also his account of the final surrender of the Japanese forces. The photographs taken during my visit to Okinawa in 1959 are credited to the U.S. Civil Administration of Ryukyu (U.S.C.A.R.).

Janet Heavenridge of the University of Hawaii Press was very instrumental in guiding me through the many technicalities of bringing my raw manuscript to final print. Her patience is much appreciated. My sister, Alice Yoshiko, was most encouraging throughout the arduous months of preparations. To the Kin Cho Jin Kai I express my appreciation for their valuable sponsorship of this book.

Introduction

The Okinawan community in Hawaii is about to celebrate the 90th anniversary of their forefathers' arrival in Hawaii. As the centerpiece, the Bunka-Kai-kan, a multi-million dollar cultural center, will be built under the auspices of the United Okinawan Association. I have written this book in the hope that it might contribute in some way to this ambitious undertaking to refurbish and sustain our cultural heritage.

This book is not intended to be a study of an ethnic or subethnic minority but merely the story of my experiences and observations as I went on a long journey through our multiethnic, interracial, internationalized world. The only justification I can advance is the fact that my journey took me to many places and gave me experiences rarely encountered by the average Nisei. By writing about these experiences, I hope to add to the literature of the second generation Japanese-Americans in Hawaii and the United States. The book does not portray a Horatio Alger success story, for I know that would be an unworthy travesty.

An autobiography, I presume, should begin with some reference to one's roots. I find this difficult and very ambiguous for I have no knowledge of my family genealogy nor any inherited stories of illustrious ancestors. The most that I can reconstruct is the old family setting in the village of Kin in the mountainous area of northern Okinawa. This area has always been referred to as *Yanbaru* and has carried the image of a mountain people, unsophisticated, rugged, and pleasure-seeking, like those people in Tennessee or Kentucky. By all accounts, my family came from a long line of peasant farmers who always struggled to survive. The economic hardships in the entire village led to an emigration to Hawaii and other parts of the world.

My parents came with the first wave of immigrants, at the turn of the century, to work on the sugar plantation in Waipahu. My father's family was large and so poor that he was not able to attend school, not even for a single year. I often wondered how painful it must have been for him to see other children frolicking off to school. My mother's family was slightly better off—she was able to go through the fourth grade in the village school.

Life on the sugar plantation was most grueling, as depicted by historians of this period such as Ernest Wakukawa, Yukiko Kimura, Yasutarō Sōga, and others. My parents left the Waipahu plantation to become pineapple homesteaders after my older brother, Yasu, and I were born, and we moved to Kahaluu Valley on the windward side of Oahu. My journey began here deep in the Koolau mountains.

From Kahaluu Valley I proceeded to Honolulu for there were no schools beyond the eighth grade on the entire windward side of Oahu. After completing my high school and university studies, my journey took me away from Hawaii for the next thirteen years: first to the University of Chicago, then to the University of Wisconsin, and finally to Detroit, Michigan, to work as an economist for the War Labor Board. I felt compelled to join the U.S. Army in 1944.

My war experiences are detailed in Chapter 5, which focuses on the Okinawa campaign. I was seriously wounded in battle and spent almost a year in military hospitals for recovery and rehabilitation.

I then returned to the University of Wisconsin to finish my doctorate in Economics. From there my journey took me to the University of Minnesota at Duluth for my first job as a professor. With the Korean War I was called to work with the National Wage Stabilization Board in Minneapolis and Washington, D.C. After this war I found my way back to Hawaii in the fall of 1953, thirteen years after I left in 1941.

The University of Hawaii was my home base for the rest of my professional career, some twenty-six years until my retirement at the age of sixty-three in 1980.

At the University I was first appointed Associate Professor in the Department of Economics. After about ten years, I transferred to the College of Business Administration in the Department of Business Economics and Quantitative Sciences. While teaching was my principal duty, I enjoyed various assignments and experiences provided by the very flexible nature of work at the University.

Within the framework of the University, I became the Director of the Economic Research Center and later the first Director of the Asian Studies Program. In 1960, along with four other colleagues from the University, I traveled through seventeen different countries of Asia to help establish contacts for the emerging East-West Center.

On leaves-of-absences from the University I enjoyed two assignments in Tokyo: first with our overseas M.B.A. program at the Tachikawa Air Force Base and later to lecture at Waseda University in Shinjuku, Tokyo. Summer session exchanges permitted me to return to the University of Wisconsin and also to teach at Xavier University in Cincinnati, Ohio.

Two other detours from my regular duty involved a research trip to the wild frontiers of Bolivia and Brazil to look into the progress of Okinawan "colonies" established there under the auspices of the U.S. Government after World War II in an effort to relieve the economic pressures on the home islands.

Another leave from my regular duty at the University took me to Washington, D.C. to serve as Administrative Assistant to U.S. Senator Daniel K. Inouye during the height of the civil rights movement.

Upon my return to Hawaii in 1964, I participated in some of the most bitter political battles experienced in the islands. The long-standing struggle within the Democratic party of Hawaii came to a climax in 1966 and again in 1970. In 1966 it was the primary fight for the seat of the Lieutenant Governor and in 1970 it was for the Governor's chair. I was campaign chairman for Thomas P. Gill in both races against Governor John A. Burns and the establishment. This is detailed in Chapter 10.

I have added, perhaps unnecessarily, a chapter entitled "Retirement Years" as a postscript to conclude my journey.

I began writing this autobiography upon reaching my seventy-second birthday. By then my mind had grown a little soft and my stamina was no longer vibrant. I ask your understanding, therefore, of my shortcomings as that of an old man steadily approaching senility.

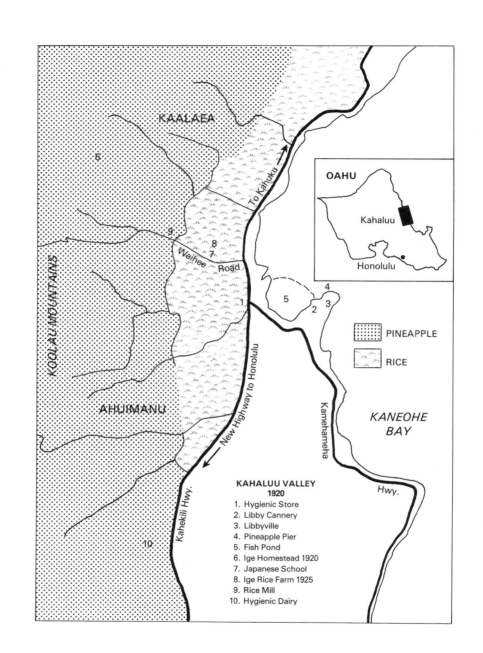

KAALAEA

To Kahuku

KOOLAU MOUNTAINS

Waihee Road

AHUIMANU

New Highway to Honolulu

Kahekili Hwy.

Kamehameha Hwy.

KANEOHE BAY

OAHU

Kahaluu

Honolulu

▨ PINEAPPLE

RICE

KAHALUU VALLEY
1920

1. Hygienic Store
2. Libby Cannery
3. Libbyville
4. Pineapple Pier
5. Fish Pond
6. Ige Homestead 1920
7. Japanese School
8. Ige Rice Farm 1925
9. Rice Mill
10. Hygienic Dairy

CHAPTER 1

Early Childhood

Kahaluu Valley

If one were going from Honolulu to Kahuku via the windward route it would be easy to pass through the town of Kahaluu without knowing it. This is because most of the houses are deep in the valley and away from Kamehameha Highway. The only landmark that you may notice is the Hygienic Store because the name is so incongruous. The story behind this unusual name is based on the acquisition of the store by the Hygienic Dairy which operated a fairly large dairy farm in the Ahuimanu section. They named the store after the dairy.

The store was originally owned by the Lau family, perhaps the most prominent family in the valley at that time. They also had cattle in the up country and a slaughterhouse that provided the only beef available, when available. As a young boy I looked forward to the branding of young calves, which was done about once a year in front of the store across the highway. In addition to the branding of the calves, young male calves were castrated and what was removed was roasted in the fire used for branding irons. They called these "mountain oysters," and I still remember how delicious they tasted.

The only other store was located across the Kahaluu stream owned by the Kanemaru family. One son, Masao, is now a prominent dentist in Wahiawa.

Okinawa Town

Perhaps the most unique feature of the valley was the predominance of those of Okinawan descent. If there was a place in

I

all Hawaii that could be called "Okinawan Town," it was Kahaluu. It was, incidentally, very appropriate that when the producers of *Karate Kid II* wanted an Okinawan village setting, they wisely chose Kahaluu. The fish pond across from the Hygienic Store was used. Many of the valley people participated in the film. I also recall they shot the picture *Bird of Paradise* with Delores Del Rio in that same fish pond when I was in the fourth grade.

Why the Okinawans settled in Kahaluu I do not know. By 1920 I believe about 80% of the one hundred households had such familiar Okinawan names as Nakama, Yogi, Asato, Higa, Afuso, Ige, Serikaku, Kogachi, Agena, Yonashiro, Kobashigawa, Kochi, Tsuha, Toguchi, Nakada, Ginoza, Kiyabu, Oshiro, Miyashiro, Yamashiro, Yamanoha, Yonamine, Gima, and so on. Because the Okinawans were such a dominant subethnic group, there was hardly any racial snobbing by the Naichi group, who were descended from Japanese from other prefectures of Japan. The occasional snubs came largely from people outside Kahaluu Valley.

There was very little reluctance in openly perpetuating the Okinawan songs and dances, pleasures that would have been frowned on elsewhere. Therefore, I became quite familiar with the Okinawan culture throughout my childhood.

There was a Christian Church in Kahaluu too. It was the Methodist Episcopal Church where I received my baptism. The reverend was a most unusual person and had a very profound effect on my life. He lived in Kaneohe and had a bigger church there as well as one in Kailua. His name was the Reverend C. P. Goto.

I clearly remember the first time I met him. It was in the Japanese school yard waiting for our classes to begin. Reverend Goto came on a bicycle all the way from Kaneohe six miles away. First he showed my friends and me some photographs of the old Asahi baseball team. He had played on the team as a pitcher prior to World War I. He couldn't have started off more auspiciously, as we were all avid baseball fans, especially of the Asahi. Later on, he taught us how to hood slide into second and third base. I used that technique throughout my baseball career. As a social institution, however, the church was no comparison to the Japanese school. Okinawans in Kahaluu basically did not take religion seriously. In my own case, however, the Reverend C. P. Goto was a prime inspiration. He later helped me to get into Mid-Pacific Institute (high school) in Honolulu.

There were a few Hawaiian families in Kahaluu living on the old Libbyville site, later St. Johns by the Sea. The largest family was the Hookanos. In the valley itself were the Kalakaua, Kukahiko, and Kawelo families. We envied them because they were small landowners, as well as citizens who could benefit from government patronage jobs and who could work for large firms such as the old Honolulu Rapid Transit Company, the Mutual Telephone Company, and Hawaiian Electric. These companies gave priority to Hawaiians and rarely hired any Nisei. Pearl Harbor and other military establishments also favored Hawaiians. In the valley the Hawaiians were more privileged than the Japanese. They had the better jobs, houses, and even automobiles. Part of the land we lived on belonged to the Kalakauas and part belonged to the Kukahiko family. The inability of these people to move up the economic ladder in later years was due, no doubt, to the fact that very few left the valley to seek higher education. There was one lonely Korean family in all of Kahaluu, the Kim family. This was a large family, but all the children were well educated. Jenny Kim became my teacher in the seventh grade at Waiahole School. I remember her fondly as the best teacher I had in elementary school.

Pineapple Cannery

Kahaluu Valley was a far more prosperous town between 1910 and 1920 than in the thirties. There was a big pineapple cannery belonging to Libby, McNiel and Libby. It was located in what was then referred to as "Libbyville," just above the fish pond; later it was called "St. Johns by the Sea." It's hard to imagine a large cannery there but we must note several facts:

One, there were numerous independent pineapple growers in the areas closer to the Koolau Mountains. My parents were among these. Two, transporting the pineapple to Honolulu from Kahaluu and the neighboring areas was very impractical since the Nuuanu Pali was barely passable. Three, a deep-water loading facility was built at the pier and a railroad ran from the cannery to the pier. This was probably the smallest railroad in the islands, something like the short rail line now running between the pineapple piers and the canneries in Iwilei. It was great fun for us kids to run through the cannery. To accommodate the cannery workers, the town of Libbyville was located right on the waterfront. I remember a small store there run by the family of Wallace Hirai, who later became known in the sports community of Hawaii as the prominent sports editor of the *Nippu Jiji*.

The lowlands of Kahaluu were filled with rice fields. A large rice mill was located almost in the center of the valley. It was run by some Chinese who had fields of their own. This mill, along with the pineapple cannery, was abandoned in the twenties, as transportation to Honolulu improved and California rice began to displace local rice. Kahaluu then began its slow decline to a sleepy community of small independent farmers who survived on a very marginal basis.

All the farmers in the valley were poor, that is, below the poverty level in today's terminology, but I can't recall a single family that went on welfare. We helped each other as the need arose. Farm families could always rely on what was available on the farm itself—sweet potatoes, taro, banana, papaya, and all kinds of vegetables. In addition, chickens and hogs were raised by the Okinawan families. Hogs were primarily for home consumption and were fed young taro leaves like those used by the Hawaiians for *lau lau*. Since taro was widely grown in Kahaluu, this food supply for the pigs was very easy to obtain throughout the year. We were, therefore, spared the humiliation of Honolulu pig farmers in gathering pig slop from neighbors. There was not a single telephone among the farmers, nor indoor plumbing. Electricity did not come in until the mid-thirties.

Japanese School

Prior to World War II, the Japanese school played a central role in almost every Japanese community in Hawaii. Kahaluu was no exception, although I had some strong but mixed feelings about the role played by the Japanese language schools in pre–World War II Hawaii. The Japanese school principal was the big "honcho," and his wife was treated like a kind of queen. Furthermore, I had a deep and abiding repugnance to this school. This feeling must have been due to the fact that I was a very poor student and suffered much ridicule throughout my eight years of attendance there. At the end of each school year, on graduation day, first, second, and third prizes were awarded for each class. In some years there were no more than five or six students in my class, yet I was never awarded even a third prize, not even once!

Graduation day was a very big day in Kahaluu Valley and the ceremonies attracted the entire Japanese community. Students were generally evaluated on the basis of their performance in the Japanese school. I was considered almost hopeless. Looking back, I feel sorry for the many embarrassments that my parents must have suffered. A major reason for my poor performance was, I believe, due to the fact that my parents had very little education and were in no position to tutor us at night. Ours was one of the few families in the valley that did not subscribe regularly to the *Nippu Jiji* or *Hawaii Hochi*, the two Japanese language dailies at that time.

New Year's Day in the valley began with ceremonies at the Japanese school. We would sing the Japanese National Anthem and bow very reverently before the picture of the Japanese emperor and empress hanging on the front wall. During speech-making by the dignitaries, almost invariably someone would relate proudly how the Japanese army was winning the war in China. Even at an early age I resented this very much, but I couldn't excuse myself since ours was the closest house to the Japanese school and we were the closest neighbor of the school principal.

Mother in a taro patch, c. 1925

Home in Kahaluu without electricity or indoor plumbing, 1925

Mother and father on the farm, c. 1935

English School

Having discussed the Japanese school, I must now add some notes on our English school. This was the Waiahole School which took in all the students from Waiahole and Waikane, in addition to Kahaluu. This school remains today as one of the oldest on Oahu. We celebrated its 100th anniversary in 1980. This school is located about a half mile in from Kamehameha Highway in Waiahole Valley. I spent my first eight years there.

The principal of the school was Alice Emogene Mudge from upstate New York. She was at Waiahole for over thirty years and was herself an institution. She was a spinster and a true curmudgeon, completely domineering.

One thing I recall about my eight years at Waiahole and that was that we never had a single male teacher. Oh, how I wished we had one! I have felt that one of the grave shortcomings of our educational system was, and is, the lack of male teachers in the lower grades.

The most vivid memory I have of those days at Waiahole was the day I got my name, Thomas. Our second grade teacher decided our given Japanese names were too cumbersome and un-American, so one day she went right down the aisle and gave us all English names: "You are John, you are William, you are Mary, you are Sheppard." When she came to me she said, "You are Thomas." I just missed being stuck with that name "Sheppard," for which I am eternally grateful. With no more to do about it, I retained the name Thomas for the rest of my life. I must agree that my Japanese name, Heihachiro, is indeed very cumbersome; ironically, the teacher's name was Miss Kamakawiwaole, even more cumbersome than my own name.

Waiahole Valley itself was very beautiful. At the deepest part was a camp for workers of the Waiahole Tunnel Company which even to this day remains a major source of water supply for the sugar plantations around Waipahu, Ewa, and Aiea. Around graduation time we were permitted to go to the mountain to gather maile for graduation leis. At the same time, we usually had a hukilau to catch fish for the graduation party. These remain happy memories.

Scholastically, I did far better in English than at the Japanese school. We had to take the Stanford Achievement Test in Honolulu during my eighth grade year, and I had the highest score. This, of course, was never known in the Japanese community of Kahaluu, where I remained a hopeless case.

An article appeared in late May 1988 in the *Honolulu Advertiser* stating that "Waiahole waltzed away with the Frito-Lay Hawaii Outstanding School award, partly in recognition of the remarkable strides it has made in math and reading scores—Principal Raymond Sugai has something to be proud of. There was a 19 percent gain in math and 7 percent gain in reading scores on the sixth graders' Stanford Achievement Tests."

The annual recognition luncheon was a chance to thank all those who had helped the school during the year. It was special for another reason. Waiahole's favorite son, state educational Superintendent Charles Toguchi, a 1956 graduate, told the students, "I was very, very proud to say that I came from Waiahole School." I, too, can say I was proud to have come from this school.

The article continued, "Forty years ago, Waiahole pupils captured Windward Coast honors in a rodent control campaign by catching the most rats—504 of them."

Baseball in Kahaluu

Here let me digress to report on the baseball team we had in Kahaluu Valley. When the Windward Oahu Japanese Senior Baseball League was organized around 1930, it was decided that Kahaluu should enter a team and this gave me my first exposure to organized baseball.

In retrospect, it appears ridiculous that Kahaluu could field a team to compete against such teams as Kahuku, a plantation team with a beautiful baseball field and strong backing from its rather large community and the plantation itself. The

Kahuku team had uniforms too. Waimanalo, on the other end of windward Oahu, was also a plantation town and, therefore, it had the benefit of good facilities and a strong players' pool. Kaneohe was a fairly large town and had the necessary manpower to field a respectable team. In addition, Kaneohe had a baseball diamond in the public park provided by the city. Kailua had to draw its players from a relatively small community and had limitations similar to those we faced in Kahaluu. However, they had some advantages we never had. They had an adequate baseball field and also had a knowledgeable manager, Isaac Iwanaga, who played shortstop for Mid-Pacific Institute in the Honolulu Interscholastic League. He was the most valuable player (MVP) the first year of the League.

In Kahaluu Valley, the baseball team was really a joke, though we didn't realize it at that time. How ridiculous we must have appeared to outsiders! Our main problem was the lack of players. Except for three or four players, the entire team was made up of boys from the surrounding farms. If all the potential players made themselves available, I suppose we could have made a decent showing, but we had trouble finding nine players on any Sunday. Only those who could be spared from duties on the farm came out. When we got into the busy seasonal periods on the farms, such as rice planting or harvesting, not too many players showed up. We tried to surmount this difficulty in several ways. When short of players, we tried to recruit others from the non-Japanese community. Players like Henry Hookano would be given a Japanese name and inserted into the lineup. I think the opposing teams were aware of our subterfuge but they seldom protested because we rarely won any games. The Koolauloa team, drawing its players from Kaaawa to Kahuku, was even worse than we were in this regard. There weren't too many Japanese living in their area so they relied heavily on outside ineligible players. Like us, they seldom won so no protests were made.

Another way of resolving the perennial problem of too few players was to recruit the young kids who were still in grammar school. This was how I first got to play, as an eighth grader playing against the older, more experienced players.

The other equally ridiculous disadvantage we had was the

lack of a suitable baseball field in the village. The best we had was the Japanese school yard on Waihee Road. From home plate to left field fence was about 260 feet. To right field, the distance was even shorter for the school itself stood on that corner. The worst aspect of playing baseball here was the big flagpole located between first and second base. All Japanese schools, as I recall, had a big flagpole as a centerpiece of their school yards.

As an eighth grader, I barely weighed a hundred pounds, but, on many occasions, I was assigned to catch for the team. I did a creditable job because I had the advantage of the flagpole. My arm was not strong enough to throw to second base when the runner attempted to steal. I solved the problem by quickly returning the ball to the pitcher, who in turn spun around and threw to second base. Ordinarily this would take too much time to catch the runner, but since the flagpole stood between first and second base, the runner had to detour slightly into right field in order to reach second. This gave me time to trap him at second base. This was something out of the Bad News Bears at its worst.

Okinawa—1923–1924

I must record a major sojourn from Kahaluu before continuing with my story. This occurred after World War I when I was six or seven years old. It was a happy occurrence with a mixture of unhappiness at the end.

My parents moved away from the plantation setting in Waipahu. We were able to settle on a pineapple homestead deep in Kahaluu Valley, so close to the mountains that that particular gulch was referred to in the very early days as "Ige Yama" next to "Higa Yama." This leased land of about thirty acres was devoted entirely to pineapple. I was too young to remember much about these early years but the record shows that this venture was a spectacular success. Money accumulated here permitted the family to realize the ultimate dream of all the early immigrants, to return to their homeland.

After joyful celebrations, our whole family set sail for Japan

Our family returned to Okinawa in 1924. *Left to right:* Yoshiko, Mother, Kosaburo, Hiroshi on father's lap, Thomas, and Yasuichi

and Okinawa. One particular obstacle delayed our departure, however—our birth certificates. None of us had any. There was no official record of birth, so our birth dates were established by going back the number of years of our ages. The difficulty with this, as I recall now, was that Japanese families always counted the baby one year old at birth, which pushed the recorded birth a year further back. This was a common occurrence, and I remember in the elementary grades we were generally one or two years older than the non-Japanese students. After much fuss and delay, we got our birth certificates, which gave us assurance of coming back to the United States.

After an arduous voyage in steerage class, we were greeted by happy relatives in Okinawa who held a celebration lasting several days. The initial joyful days were followed by some dubious developments. Relatives borrowed heavily from the "rich one just returned from Hawaii." It must have been difficult for my parents to deny any request as all our relatives were poor and struggling. Because of all of these loans, our remaining assets quickly evaporated.

My older brother, Yasu, and I had to adjust to the new school environment in the village of Kin in northern Okinawa. I was then in the second grade. Though I was never a good student in the Japanese school in Hawaii, in the Kin Village school my deficiency became more pronounced. The second grade students there, as well as in all of Okinawa and Japan, were far more advanced than second graders in Hawaii. After all, they spent all day learning Japanese, whereas in Hawaii we spent no more than an hour a day learning the language. The other students began calling me pumpkin, *bobula*. My brother and I were very unhappy and wished we had never left Hawaii. I finally returned after a year, and my brother and our entire family came back later. Our family fortune was almost completely depleted. To me, this was a classic example of exploding a myth held by early immigrants that they would make a fortune overseas and return back to the life of "happy ever after" in their old country.

This brief sojourn, however, permitted me to observe and enjoy other aspects of village life in old Okinawa. In so many ways, the village life there was far richer than that in Hawaii. You lived in the atmosphere of a town setting which was hundreds of years old. Traditions and customs meant so much to the villagers who were all racially the same and who shared a common history. The music and dances were handed down through the generations and they had the richness lacking in the more cosmopolitan setting of Hawaii. For example, there was the annual "Tsuna Hiki" held in the village. This tug-of-war was celebrated with much gusto and involved the entire village community in the weaving together of the giant rope. Mass participation was an expected part of all main events.

In Kahaluu the farmers' homes and fields were scattered over a very wide area. In Kin Village, although the fields were scattered in the same way, the homes and the farmers were all centered in a town not unlike the plantation camp in Hawaii. This permitted a social life far richer than the unstructured hit-and-miss socializing found in Kahaluu and other farm

OKINAWA

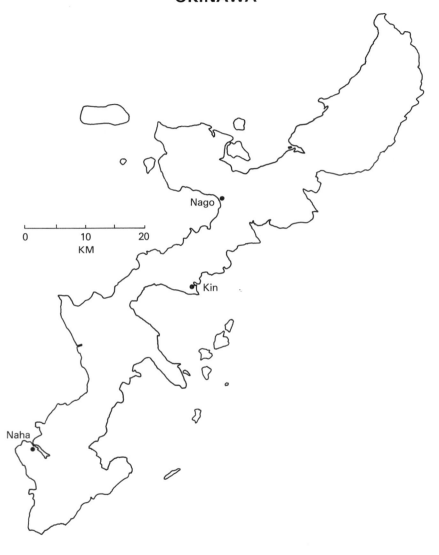

areas of Hawaii. Within this town setting of Kin, the social center was the school, the village office, and, most importantly, the village spring. The spring was something quite special and unique to Kin Village. It was more than a central source of water. The spring was wide and deep and contained many sections. One section was enclosed for showers, another was for getting fresh drinking water, a third was for washing vegetables and clothes, and the last was for washing animals. The spring water there was so clear and sweet that villagers came from far away places to take some of the water home. Adjoining the spring was the community bath house. None of my relatives' homes, as I recall, had bathing facilities. They all came to this *furo*, which cost them only a few pennies. The social life evolving around this water hole referred to by the villagers as *"Ō-Kawa,"* the big river, was all-encompassing. As kids, if we had nothing to do, we always went and "got some action" at the *Ō-Kawa*.

The after-school activities there bring back many happy memories of childhood days. It was common for a group of

The spring in Kin Village

boys to get together and go into the mountains to gather pine needles and firewood. We took big wicker baskets on our backs and also brought back grass cuttings for the goats and pigs. We frolicked along the way in the Huckleberry Finn–Tom Sawyer manner as we crossed rivers and meadows into the mountains. I can't recall a single incident of this kind in Kahaluu.

My dad would tell us stories of his days in Kin where young people, both boys and girls, gathered occasionally in some choice spot in the meadows and would spend the evening in song and dance. This was referred to as *mo asubi*, or playing in the meadows. The playing of the Okinawan *samisen* was also an integral part of these parties. I think the songs, dances, and the playing of the *samisen* that followed the immigrants to Hawaii had their roots in the meadows of the Okinawan villages.

One other point of interest in Kin Village, then and now, is the statue of Kyuzo Toyama in the center of the village. The statue itself is perched on top of a long (100 steps) cement stairway going up the hillside. The right arm of the Toyama statue is outstretched like that of the King Kamehameha statue in Honolulu, urging his countrymen to go overseas. It is in the spirit that Horace Greeley advised "Go West, young man, go West" before the turn of the century in our own country. Funds to build this statue of Toyama were largely obtained by donations from Okinawans overseas before the war in appreciation of Toyama's foresight. During World War II the Japanese melted down the statue to use the scrap for war materials. It was rebuilt again after the war and will stand forever as a symbol of friendship and goodwill to the rest of the world.

When we returned to Hawaii from Okinawa in 1925, we bought a leasehold farm of almost ten acres behind the Japanese school. We lived practically in the center of the valley. Most of the farm was devoted to rice and later to taro but papaya, banana, and sweet potatoes were grown in the drier section. My folks lived on the same farm until the 1960s, all through my high school and university days. We bought the land in the fifties, and my brother Kosaburo still owns and lives on part of this land.

CHAPTER 2

Off to Honolulu
1932

Central Intermediate School—1932

Two from our graduating class of fifteen at Waiahole School went on to Central Intermediate School. Attending a big city school for the first time was a traumatic experience for a country boy, at least for the first few months. For the first time I was exposed to changing classes and teachers with every subject I took. Lunch hour was also a big deal for me because we all went to the school cafeteria for our lunch. This was exhilarating! In grammar school we brought our own lunches and ate by ourselves. Also, the physical education period was most exciting for we participated in all sorts of activities, and I gradually gained confidence and believed I could keep up with the students from the big city. This was really a big step for a country boy who had a decided inferiority complex.

I commuted every day from Kahaluu to Central Intermediate. There were no public schools beyond the eighth grade in the entire windward district. Central was the closest school but it was twenty miles away. We had to drive through the Nuuanu Pali every day. Though the drive was picturesque and refreshing, it was, nonetheless, a great inconvenience.

The only vivid recollection I have from my year at Central was the Armistice Day parade. We had to march from Fort DeRussy at the north end of Waikiki through the heart of Waikiki to Kapiolani Park. The distance we had to march was not as much of a problem as was the requirement that we all had to wear shoes. We never wore shoes up to then and I didn't even own a pair. I bought a brand new pair and attempted to march. After about three blocks, both my feet were so blistered that I was limping quite badly. I finally had to take the shoes off in order to continue. Carrying my shoes, I made it the rest of the way. I can well imagine the amusement of the spectators lining Kalakaua Avenue, but the boy from Kahaluu had to make the best of a painful situation.

Mid-Pacific Institute—1933–1936

After one year of torturous commuting to Central Intermediate, my next three years was spent at Mid-Pacific Institute, a boarding school. The twenty-four hour association with fellow students from all over the Territory was an exciting and memorable experience for me. The total cost, including tuition, room, and board, was $225 a year in the mid-thirties. Obviously, Mid-Pacific was heavily subsidized by supporting Christian families like the Damiens, Athertons, Wilcoxes, and others.

Mid-Pacific Institute

The location of the school itself was excellent. We could walk down to Moiliili for an occasional saimin snack or to the Honolulu Stadium for football or baseball games. Bordering the University of Hawaii on the mauka side were the streetcar and later the bus lines, which easily connected to all parts of the city. The school was coeducational from junior high through high school. Being a relatively small school of about two hundred students, classes were small and we got to know each other like brothers and sisters.

Most of us had work scholarships that paid for about half of our total expenses. We did our own laundry, which was a completely new experience. I would have to say, however, we were somewhat backward socially. Not only were most of us from poor rural areas, but the traditional oriental reserve also prevented us from enjoying the kind of social intercourse found in typical American high schools. I never had a single date during my entire three years. School dances were infrequent and not much fun. The dining facilities were strictly segregated as were the living accommodations.

Despite these limitations, close bonds with a few students did have some lasting value for me. The single most important friendship I made there was with Harry Oshima who became my lifelong companion. We shared a dormitory room during my first year at Mid-Pacific; we debated together on the University freshmen team; we stayed in close contact while in graduate school; and, finally, we were fellow professors in the Department of Economics at the University of Hawaii. He was, in my estimation, one of the most brilliant of all the Niseis I knew in Hawaii. His background was most fascinating. His family owned a restaurant on Beretania Street near the corner of River Street in what was then referred to as Tin Can Alley. This was part of Honolulu's notorious red-light district, and I could easily see why his parents wanted him away from there and in a Christian boarding school.

During the period of World War I and the twenties, Mid-Pacific was known for its strong baseball tradition with stars like Kenzo Nushida, Zenimura and Ken Yen Chun. They took several championships in the Interscholastic League of Honolulu during that period. From the middle twenties baseball

sagged badly and Mid-Pacific Institute was relegated to the
Junior Scholastic League. About 1933 a concerted effort was
made to revitalize the sport.

To this end, Mid-Pacific's first move was to hire as head
coach "Kaiser" Tanaka, one of the leading and best known
players of that period. He starred for many years with the
Asahi ball club and was one of my childhood heroes. Kaiser
immediately recruited two brothers from the well-known
Kameda baseball family in Wailua, Shigeo and Toshio, as
shortstop and pitcher respectively. From the Inoshita family
in Waipahu he took on Masao (Crane) for first base, from the
Kashiwaeda family on Kauai, Hifumi (Blackie) played third
base, and Donald Miura came from Kapaa, Kauai, to play
infield. I was most anxious to become a part of this revitaliza-
tion and I especially wanted to learn to catch from the great
Kaiser Tanaka.

In the end, however, this was a big disappointment—a personal disaster. The team never became a serious contender in
the league which was dominated by St. Louis and McKinley. I
made the varsity team as a sophomore but I sat on the bench
the entire time I was on the team. This in itself, I think, was
some kind of a record: no at-bats, no hits, one run scored. It
was in the last game of my last season, when the team had
nothing at stake in a game against Kamehameha on our home
field, that the final insult occurred. In the final inning of the
game, Kaiser, to my surprise, finally called out my name as I
was quietly warming the bench. I jumped up in glee and went
for a long-awaited first time at bat. As I selected my bat, I was
told to pinch run for the runner already on first base. With my
head down, I made it to first base and I finally scored a run. As
the entire student body knew of my ignominious record in the
ball club, they gave me a big hand as I crossed the plate. It was
most embarrassing for me, and the deep hurt I felt stayed with
me for many years afterwards. In retrospect, this made me
more determined than ever to prove myself as a baseball
player.

During summer vacations in high school I worked on a
pineapple plantation in Wahiawa, Camp 9 (Pomoho), run by
the California Packing Corporation (CPC). It was a fairly large

camp of about fifty families, mostly Japanese, with some Filipino bachelors. Pineapple growing was very seasonal then, and during the peak summer months the number of employees doubled. Regular employees lived in company houses. A company store provided most of the necessities, for hardly anyone owned a car to drive into the nearby town of Wahiawa to buy goods. A free bathhouse was also provided. In addition, there was a fairly large and good baseball diamond right in the camp compound.

The head man at this camp was Mr. Ginki Ikehara. He was also field superintendent, and he had the biggest and best house in the camp. I was very fond of him for several reasons. He was an Okinawan from the same village of Kin as my own parents so we had known him long before I worked at this camp. Beyond any doubt, he had the most prestigious job of all the people known to my family. I was quietly proud to see him driving around in a nice car provided by the company, with a safari-type hat worn by the big shots. He was also a prominent leader in the town of Wahiawa and he strongly supported many of its activities, especially baseball. He was well liked and highly respected by everyone.

After almost a lifetime of service with the pineapple company, Mr. Ikehara finally decided to retire. Ironically and tragically he died on the very last day of service. He must have been emotionally overcome. We might say he literally died with his boots on.

This summer experience gave me a good opportunity to observe life in a pineapple camp and to compare it to the life of farmers in Kahaluu Valley. Socially the camp life was far superior to living in the country. The community bath, in particular, not only provided welcome relief from the long day's work in the hot sun but also the opportunity to socialize. In the recollection of the Isseis, life on the plantation was almost always portrayed as grim and exploitative. No doubt, there were grievous injustices on the pineapple and sugar plantations, though I was not aware of them at that time. One needs only to read about the general strikes that occurred in the twenties to understand why so many families left the plantation for life in town and for the freedom of the countryside,

Robert Taira

eventually to participate in the formation of a strong labor union on all the islands. The economic structure of the plantation was a classic case of what is known in economics as "monopsony" and "oligopsony," where exclusive power is centered in one or a few large companies acting in collusion. The power here was on the buyers' side instead of the side of the sellers. The companies bought labor services. The wage rates and working conditions were virtually identical on all the plantations. At the time I worked in the camp, I was paid 17½ cents an hour, the same in all camps of the big three companies.

During my high school and college days, my idol and role model was Robert Taira, who graduated three years ahead of me. The fact that he too was of Okinawan descent may have had some influence on me. He was the "big man on campus," excelling academically as well as athletically. Physically he was very handsome and he was also very gracious in his relationships with others. While we were struggling through high school, Robert Taira was making a name for himself at the University. He received much publicity and praise in making the all-university debate team, which successfully toured the West Coast. He also held class offices. I remember how resplendent he looked in his R.O.T.C. officer's uniform with a saber at his side. Because our high school was practically on

Thomas Ige was presented the Ah Shin
Ching, 18″ silver trophy for outstanding
service to Mid-Pacific Institute

the University of Hawaii campus, we followed closely whatever transpired there. Robert later served with distinction in
World War II battles in Europe and then he became a prominent leader in our state senate.

I finished high school as president of the student body and
received an outstanding service award. However, I must
frankly admit that I was not an outstanding student and had
no particular talent in any field. My future at the University
did not seem too bright or promising.

University of Hawaii—1936–1940

For the second generation of any ethnic minority, the University of Hawaii was a crucial step on the path to the upper levels of society. The University was sacrosanct. It commanded
great respect among the first generation of immigrants. For
many, it was considered beyond the reach of their own chil-

Hawaii Union. *First row:* Howard Miyake, Harold Wright. *Second row:* Richard Okamoto, Robert Ho. *Third row:* Mineo Katagiri, William Charman. *Fourth row:* Harry Oshima, Thomas Ige

dren. As in Japan, education was a top priority, and families were more than willing to make great sacrifices to send even one of their children to college. No one from Kahaluu had ever gone to the University until the mid-thirties. First to go were three boys who had attended Mid-Pacific Institute a year ahead of me, Shigeo Kobashigawa, David Higa, and Chester Zukeran. All three were of Okinawan descent. I followed next and Roy Nakada attended right after me.

For me, entering the University was made easy—almost automatic—due to a series of fortuitous events. While in high school I taught Sunday School at the Manoa Mission, a few blocks mauka of Mid-Pacific. The school was run by Mrs. Sumi Yoshioka. Without my knowledge, she enlisted the support of Mrs. Alexander Johnston Ross, one of the pillars of the Mission, to give me a scholarship. Her husband, Dr. Ross, was a professor of theology at Harvard University. I considered this unexpected good fortune the first of several blessings I received serendipitously. I am forever indebted to Mrs. Yoshioka for this.

Having entered the University, it was difficult for me to decide on a major. I was neither gifted nor interested in any particular field of study. For the first two years this indecision did not present problems for we generally took the same basic required courses. From my junior year until I graduated I majored in Social Science with no specific focus. I took elective courses in Economics, Political Science, History, Sociology, Philosophy, and Literature. None of these courses were intended to prepare me for any specific vocation or profession. I used to get greatly embarrassed when my parents and their friends asked me what I was doing at the University. I had no goal or focus; I was only enriching my background for God knows what. Though I was in the process of finding myself, it was difficult to explain this to my parents who were struggling heroically on the farm. I was most grateful for their patience and understanding while I was very unsure of myself but, nevertheless, doing my best. In retrospect, the broad spectrum of courses I took was most helpful in my teaching profession, and I have no regrets.

I was also involved with activities and developments be-

yond the University campus. The labor movement in Hawaii
began to stir the rigid structure of the established oligarchy.
The New Deal was the new hope of a depression-borne generation. We were swept into the liberalism that was fast emerging among the young students from the plantation and the
rural farms. I spent many hours attending labor rallies involving the stevedores on the waterfront, as well as attending
court cases in Honolulu where Filipino labor leaders on Maui
were being tried for "conspiracy." For me, these were as educational as classroom lectures.

In my first year at the University, my buddy, Harry Oshima, won the all-University oratorical contest as a freshman.
This was most noteworthy, for he blasted the oligarchy in no
uncertain terms. There were responses from the Big Five
downtown who generally ignored student activities at the
University. A few years later, George Fukuoka, who eventually became a state senator and judge, criticized the close-knit
operation of the student government run by the Honolulu student leaders. One could sense the beginning of rebellion as

The University of Hawaii "H" Club (Organization for Sports Lettermen).
Row one, left to right: H. Chock, H. Blake, W. Mookini, J. Kaulukukui,
A. Lee, T. Ige. *Row two:* M. Abreu, R. Sekiya, W. Richardson, U. Uchima,
W. Meyer, S. Tanaka. *Row three:* S. Watasaki, K. Otagaki, G. Greenwell,
L. Louis, E. Lam, V. Dang, F. Kauka

students from the other islands, as well as those from the rural and slum areas of Honolulu, began to assert themselves.

We non-Honolulu students were faced with the problem of finding living quarters. I started off at the Okumura Dorm run by Reverend Takie Okumura and his family. The dorm was affiliated with the castle-like Makiki church. All the residents, about forty or fifty of us, including girls, attended either nearby McKinley High School or the University. After one semester I left to join students who independently rented and operated their own houses. These houses were spread out near the University in the Moiliili, McCully, and the Bingham Tract areas. In these houses we developed friendships and associations that would last a lifetime, similiar to the old school ties of the Ivy League universities on the East Coast.

Consciously, or unconsciously, a sense of rebellion began developing as the depression was still with us as were memories of our plantation rural life. Consequently, out of these "poor boy houses" emerged some of the leaders who were to reshape Hawaiian society in the post-war period. Some of their names are quite familiar now—former state senator Najo Yoshinaga; George Fukuoka; Spark Matsunaga; Sakae Takahashi; house speaker Tadao Beppu; Dan Aoki, Governor Burns' right arm; Angel Maehara, Mayor Blaisdell's leader; Yoshimi Shimizu, the Major's finance director; circuit court judges Toshio Kabatan and Casey Hige; and federal bankruptcy judge Jon Chinen. Many became doctors or lawyers and in the post-war period played prominent roles in the emergence of the new Democratic Party.

There was little political activity on the University campus, even though we were inexorably drifting toward World War II. We all had our draft-board numbers and, sheep-like, we awaited our call. Even the professors kept a quiet stance, unlike the turmoil of the Vietnam era.

Graduating from the University in June 1940, it was a most difficult time to find a job. The depression was not quite over, the military draft hung heavily over our heads, and employers were reluctant to take us on a temporary basis. I was most fortunate to land a job with the Matson Navigation Company as a clerk on the waterfront. The job was given to me not

Ajimine, Yoshishige
Kailua, Oahu

Beppu, Tadao
Kahaluu, Oahu

Ige, Thomas
Kahaluu, Oahu

Kobashigawa, Shigeo
Kahaluu, Oahu

Miyasato, Lawrence
Kapaa, Kauai

Ono, Tokuji
Honolulu

Oshima, Harry T.
Honolulu

Shimizu, Yoshimi
Kilauea, Kauai

Tanaka, Susumu
Waialua, Oahu

Teruya, Kenrichi
Wailuku, Maui

Graduation from the University of Hawaii,
June 1940

because of my university training but because I was a baseball
player. Matson had a team in the Honolulu Commercial
League, a high-powered league which played all its games in
the Honolulu Stadium for which admission was charged.
About half the players on the Matson team were from the
Asahi ball club of the Hawaii League—Matsuo Fujii, Hideo
Hioki, Sus Takana, Joe Takata, Ewa Okuda, and Goro Moriguchi. Since I too was with the Asahi ball club, I was invited
to join them.

CHAPTER 3

Baseball
1937–1940

It may appear pretentious for me to devote a whole chapter to baseball. Though I was never an outstanding baseball player, baseball was a vital part of the life of the Niseis in the pre–World War II days in Hawaii. It was equally as important to the Japanese communities throughout the islands. As a social force, it united the first- and second-generation Japanese in Hawaii in a very healthy, dynamic way. The older generations, without any other form of recreational activity, looked forward to the baseball games on Sundays and saw them as a welcome relief from their workaday grind, as well as a wholesome outlet for their pent-up emotions. No other social institution helped to bridge the gap between the Isseis and Niseis as baseball did in the twenties and thirties in Hawaii.

In my own family my dad became a devoted baseball fan ever since his plantation days in Waipahu. He encouraged us in the sport, buying us baseball equipment and taking us to games at an early age. No discussion in our family was as animated as the discussions on the many phases of baseball. I'm sure this was true for many families, as baseball was a favorite topic of conversation in any social gathering.

Baseball was played on many different levels in Hawaii. The Japanese Senior Baseball Leagues operating on all the islands were well organized and highly competitive. Their activities were duly reported every week in both the Japanese dailies, the *Nippu Jiji* and the *Hawaii Hochi*. Wallace Hirai and Monte Ito, sports editors of the respective papers, were well known and respected in the Japanese community. The

Star Bulletin and the *Advertiser* were just as meticulous in following the league games. For the first time, this kind of wide publicity gave the Japanese community a unique sense of identity and pride in their various teams. Not only the weekly box scores but also the league standings and batting averages appeared regularly, and the names of outstanding players became familiar throughout the entire territory.

In Honolulu the Japanese Senior Baseball League was organized somewhat along geographic lines. There were large Japanese communities in Moiliili, Palama, Kakaako, McCully, and the north-east areas of Honolulu, and the baseball teams were the central focus in these areas, easily surpassing the Japanese schools in interest and importance. Other teams, such as Koyu Kai (Kalihi), Seibus (Liliha), and Nippon (River Street), were loosely based, again along geographic lines. In later years, teams became less and less restrictive in this regard as the population became more and more mobile. Wahiawa was the only non-Honolulu team in this league.

In the Honolulu Japanese Senior League, I first played for the Palama team, though I never lived in the Palama area. In 1937, it happened that Haru Uchimura, the main pitcher for Palama, was also the No. 1 pitcher for the University of Hawaii baseball team. I was his chief reliever and after my first season as a freshman, he recommended me to the Palama ball club. As the club already had two strong pitchers in Seichi "Japanese" Tsugawa and Goro Moriguchi, my year with them was spent mainly on the bench. That year Palama took the Territorial championship with outstanding performances by "Taboots" Eguchi, Manabe, Charley Yoda, Kay Enomoto, Reiban Kawamoto, Masuto Fujii, Specs Ikegami, Hioka, and Mike Miike. "Wop" Shimagawa was the coach.

Azuma—1938–1940

In 1938, the following season, I joined the Azuma ball club. It was a relatively young team, made up primarily of University boys. Since we had our practice sessions on the University

Azuma's baseball team. Members of the team are: *Front row, left to right:* Tokio Hamai, Tatsuo Tokushi, Robert Higashino, George Higashino, mascot; Takeshi Kimura, Hiroshi Watanabe, Mineo Katagiri. *Second row:* Yoshiharu Ono, Richard Yoshimura, Susumu Tanaka, M. Yamashita, Y. Hashimoto, Tadao Murashige, Toshio Kameda, Francis Funai, coach. *Third row:* Aoki, Tom Ige, Dr. Yorio Wakatake, president; George Ikeno, Stanley Saiki, James Miyamura, assistant manager and coach; Tadao Takeuchi, manager, Takemi Sakaue, Mike Kinoshita

field, it was convenient for me to be with them. For the first time in the history of Japanese baseball in Hawaii, University boys made up the bulk of any team. Since the mid-thirties, high school Nisei ball players began going to the University. This, I believe, made many otherwise neutral fans cheer for us. Also, there was the unique presence of many neighbor island boys playing on the Azuma team. From Kauai we had Don Miura, Stanley Saiki, Kozuo Takanishi, and Tadao Murashige; from Maui, Tadao Beppu, Angel Maehara, and Mike Kinoshita. From Oahu we had several players: Ikeno and Fred Ida from Kailua; George Fuji from Kaneohe; Sus Tanaka from

Waialua; M. Kataguri from Haleiwa; Dan Konno and Uchigaki from Waipahu. Honolulu-bred boys made up the remain-
der: Ed Kitamura, Richard Yoshimura, Ken Hamai, and Woody
Katsumura. We were fortunate to have a strong core of back-
ers in Dr. Yorio Wakatake, president of the club, James Miyamura, Y. Hashimoto, Tai Miyamura, Dr. Mitsuda, George
Hasegawa, George Higashino, E. M. Kato, and "Council"
Takeuchi. Because we did not have the kind of community
support enjoyed by such teams as Moiliili and Kakaako, their
generous individual support was badly needed and much
appreciated.

Francis Funai was the guiding genius of the club and in two
years he was able to build a motley crew into league champions. In his quiet and gentle way, he was able to inspire the
kind of cooperation and effort we gladly gave. He tried me as a
pitcher behind Toshi Kameda the first year but I got "busted"
quite often, so he shifted me to the outfield because my bat
was more effective than my arm. It was as an outfielder that I
played most of the games with Azuma.

My most memorable game during our championship year
in 1940 was the one against a strong Moiliili ball club. Funai
unfortunately started me off as his pitcher. I got "bombed"
inside the three innings, so he put me in right field to replace
my buddy, Tadao Beppu. By the seventh inning we were still
behind by three runs. In the ensuing innings we rallied for
four runs and won in spectacular fashion. I connected for
three successive doubles in three successive innings to win
the game, some kind of record at the old stadium.

As champions of the Honolulu League we entered the Territorial Championship Tournament at the Honolulu Stadium.
In the decisive game that would determine the Oahu team
that would battle the neighbor island team, we met the powerful rural Oahu champions from Waialua. After a hard-fought
battle, we lost 4 to 3 in the last inning. Waialua finally won
the territorial championship, defeating Kauai in the title
game. This was no surprise since on a man-for-man basis,
Waialua was far superior to the rest of the field. They had several Hawaii League-caliber players in Charley Taketa, Chereet

Takata, Joe Takata, and Cooper Tanaka. They also had stars from other rural teams, like Higuchi from Pearl City and Lefty Ohira and Miyagi from Aiea, with whom they took the Territorial championship.

For me, this game was my final crowning glory, as I was soon to leave for the mainland. I felt that I played the best game of my life. Furthermore, I was soon to join the Asahi ball club. Adding to my joy was the presence of a strong delegation that included my entire family and folks from my old home town in Kahaluu. There were over seven thousand fans in the stands, and the game was given territory-wide radio coverage.

Throughout my Azuma days I felt that coach Funai generously gave me more opportunities than I rightfully deserved. Coming after my utter frustration with my high school coach, Kaiser Tanaka, I was more appreciative than coach Funai could have imagined.

Asahi—1940

To make the Asahi ball club was the ultimate dream of all Nisei baseball players in the pre-war period. Out of hundreds of young men, only about two dozen were chosen to play in the Hawaii League. This league was made up of the ever powerful Braves (mostly Portuguese boys), the Chinese team, the Hawaiians, the Wanderers (the supposedly "haole" team), and the Sub-Pac team out of Pearl Harbor. The league began its schedule after the Japanese, Chinese, and other leagues finished their seasons, which was around the end of May continuing through August.

I played only one season in 1940 before leaving for graduate work on the mainland. I was very proud to wear the Asahi uniform and to play in most games. Here again, I thought the coach, Allen Nagata, was more than fair to me, letting me play when players much better than I was were sitting on the bench. I did, however, make the Rookie All-Star Team which was as good as I could have hoped for.

A highlight of my only year with Asahi was the game

Azumas Rout Pals 7-0!
Moiliilis 6-5! Kakaakos

By WALLACE HIRAI

AZUMA

	AB	R	BH	PO	A	E
D. Konno, ss	5	1	2	1	3	0
R. Yoshimura, 3b	5	0	0	0	1	0
G. Ikeno, c	3	2	2	3	1	0
S. Tanaka, 1b	5	1	3	9	0	0
T. Ige, lf	5	0	2	2	0	1
G. Fujii, rf	4	0	1	0	0	0
T. Beppu, cf	2	1	0	3	0	0
D. Miura, 2b	4	1	1	4	1	1
E. Kitamura, p	4	0	0	3	2	0
W. Katsunuma, cf	1	1	0	2	0	0
Totals	38	7	11	27	8	2

PALAMA

	AB	R	BH	PO	A	E
S. Tokioka, lf	4	0	1	2	0	0
M. Fujii, cf	4	0	1	1	0	0
H. Yoda, ss	3	0	1	1	0	0
K. Eguchi, 1b	3	0	1	13	0	0
H. Yamashita, rf	4	0	0	1	0	0
R. Kawamoto, 3b	2	0	0	2	2	0
K. Enomoto, 2b	4	0	0	1	7	1
M. Miike, c	3	0	0	5	1	0
S. Tsugawa, p	0	0	0	0	0	0
G. Moriguchi, p	2	0	0	1	1	0
D. Matsumura, p	1	0	0	0	0	0
Totals	30	0	3	27	12	1

Hits and Runs by Innings

Azuma	110	000	230—	7
Basehits	310	010	231—	11
Palama	000	000	000—	0
Basehits	100	011	000—	3

SUMMARY—Left on bases, Azuma 10, Palama 7! Runs batted in: by Ige 3, Konno, Yoshimura, Ikeno; Two-base hits: Eguchi, S. Tanaka, G. Fujii; Sacrifice hit: Miura; Stolen base: M. Fujii; Double play: Kitamura to Tanaka; Hit by pitcher: Beppu, Matsumura; Bases on balls: off Kitamura 4; off Moriguchi 4; Struck out: by Kitamura 2; by Moriguchi 5; Umpires: Mladinich, Itoga; Time of game: 1:55.

LEAGUE STANDING

	W.	L.	Pct.
Kakaako	4	1	.800
Azuma	3	1	.750
Palama	3	2	.600
Moiliili	3	2	.600
Wahiawa	2	2	.500
Koyu	2	3	.400
Nippon	1	3	.250
Seibu	0	4	.000

AZUMA-PALAMA

The day's biggest feature easily was Pitcher Ed Kitamura's shutout pitching against the mighty Palamas who, as in their previous contest against the Moiliilis, were in a deep rut.

With his slow and tantalizing curves working as he ordered them, Kitamura had no trouble snuffing out the champions. Issuing only three scattered hits, Ed kept out of trouble throughout the nine innings.

Good support by his teammates, both defensively and offensively, went a long way towards making Eddie the winning pitcher over Palama's entire staff of Seichi Tsugawa, Goro Moriguchi and "Dopey" Matsumura.

While Pal stickers were constantly kept guessing at the offerings of the Azuma slow-baller, the young redshirts pounced on the Pal chuckers for a total of 11 bingles.

Tom Hits Effectively

Funai's cohorts banged away as if they had no respect for Palama's fine array of twirlers, and leading the attack were lanky Tom Ige, a former Pal, with two bingles and three runs driven in, and Capt. Sus Tanaka, with three out of five. George Ikeno and Dan Konno were other A's who connected for two each.

The Funais wasted no time in taking the lead, shooting home the first run in the very first canto. After two hands were gone, Ikeno, Tanaka and Ige hit consecutively and George tallied. Tom Ige's bingle finished Tsugawa, and Moriguchi, who subsequently was to suffer the same fate in the eighth, relieved him.

In the lower half of the same frame, after two outs, Hitoshi Yoda walked. Taboots Eguchi lashed out a double. Neither runner scored because Hide Yamashita, usually dangerous in the clutch, failed to deliver. He flied out to Firstbaseman Tanaka.

Finishing Touches in Eighth

Konno's single netted Beppu in the second, then in the seventh Tanaka's double and Ige's single brought in two more markers. The A's then applied the finishing touches in the eighth.

Azumas Repeat Over Moiliilis

Banzai, Azuma!

MOILIILI	AB	R	BH	PO	A	E
T. Omiya, 2b	2	1	1	0	4	0
S. Akita, ss	3	0	1	2	2	1
Monji, rf	5	0	1	1	0	1
Nakai, cf	4	2	2	2	0	0
Takeuchi, 3b	5	0	2	0	0	0
Ohta, 1b	4	0	1	12	0	0
Nakamura, c	5	0	1	6	1	0
Okada, p	3	0	1	0	2	0
Tagawa, lf	3	0	1	0	0	2
Nekota, lf	2	0	0	1	0	0
Suzuki, p	1	0	1	0	0	0
Totals	37	3	12	24	9	4
AZUMA	AB	R	BH	PO	A	E
Konno, ss	3	0	0	2	2	2
Ige, lf	4	1	1	3	0	0
Ikeno, c	4	0	0	3	0	1
Tanaka, 1b	3	1	1	9	1	0
Yoshimura, 3b	3	1	1	0	2	0
Fujii, rf	4	0	0	1	0	0
Beppu, cf	3	1	2	4	0	0
Miura, 2b	3	0	0	5	2	0
Uchigaki, p	2	0	0	0	4	0
Totals	29	4	5	27	10	3

Hits and Runs by Innings

Moiliili	100	001	001— 3
Basehits	002	013	123—12
Azuma	000	012	00x— 4
Basehits	000	014	00x— 5

By WALLACE HIRAI

Though outhit by seven bingles, the Azumas yesterday made the most of their five measly safeties and clever base running to edge out the Moiliilis and at the same time clinch the 1940 Honolulu Japanese Senior baseball championship.

The titular contest, waged at the Stadium, attracted a large gathering of over 3,000 spectators. Final score of the thrill-packed melee was 4 to 3, identical with the count of the previous battle between these arch rivals.

By dint of their brilliant victory, the Francis Funai-coached Redshirts will represent the league in the annual territorial tournament to be held at the Stadium April 20-21.

For the A's, incidentally, this marks their fifth league championship since the circuit was organized in 1924, and they're now tied with the Moiliilis for the most number of championships won.

TOM IGE

Ige, Tanaka Hit Hard to Spark A's 11-10 Mastery of Elephants

By MONTE ITO

The champion Palamas didn't have a spot for the slender, willowy righthander from Kaaawa but the Azumas did, and Thomas Ige today is the toast of the A's.

Yesterday he started on the mound for Azuma in a Honolulu Senior Japanese Baseball league tussle against the Moiliili White Elephants, was blasted off the mound, but retaliated with heavy bludgeon work to lead the A's to a sensational 11 to 10 victory.

Played before a scattering of fans at the Stadium in the morning, Coach "Funny" Funai's Azuma "collegians" waged a terrific uphill battle to wrest the hard earned victory.

Trailing 9 to 3 going into the sixth inning, the A's suddenly found their bearings and literally pounded and smashed their way to a glorious finish by scoring eight runs in three innings. And the mighty hitting of Tom Ige, tore out three successive doubles in successive innings, was the beacon that blazed brightest for the Azumas.

Tanaka Helps, Too

Then there was big Sus Tanaka, Azuma's minute-man in the hour of need, whose resounding triple scored the two runs that deadlocked the count. Also, Minoru Kinoshita, Azuma's center fielder, must not be forgotten. It was his dynamic home run in the sixth that gave vent to the A's triumphant drive.

Some measure of credit must be given to Toshi Kameda, too. The A's southpaw ace bore down with invincible power in the last two innings after troubled chapters since he relieved Ige in the third.

The final issue was decided in the eighth inning. The Moiliilis were ahead, 10-8. With one gone, Mineo Katagiri singled for his first hit of the game. Pitcher Seiko Nakasone then beaned Kimura to put himself in a hole. Up came Sus Tanaka to make glory with his triple to score the tying runs. Kinoshita followed, but grounded out weakly. Came Ige's turn, who in the preceding two innings had connected for doubles, and the Palama castoff became the hero by duplicating his two-bagger feats, driving in Tanaka with the payoff run.

"Tom Ige, (who) tore out three successive doubles in successive innings . . ."

Sports In Miniature

By MONTE ITO

HONOLULU JAPANESE SENIOR BASEBALL LEAGUE ALL-STAR TEAMS

S. Tanaka   T. Omiya   I. Mamiya   T. Takeuchi

FIRST TEAM		SECOND TEAM
Goro Moriguchi (P)	P	Toshi Kameda (A)
Seichi Tsugawa (P)	P	Ita Kurata (N)
Kazuo Masui (S)	P	Lefty Okada (M)
Riyoichi Kawamoto (P)	C	Noboru Miike (P)
Susumu Tanaka (A)	1B	Tadashi Ohta (M)
Tsuneo Omiya (M)	2B	Noboru Manabe (P)
Takeo Takeuchi (M)	3B	Jim Hironaka (N)
Iwa Mamiya (S)	SS	Joe Takata (N)
Masuto Fujii (P)	OF	Iwao Ikegami (P)
Masao Nakai (M)	OF	George Miyagawa (N)
Hideo Yamashita (S)	OF	Tom Ige (A)

M. Fujii   P. Nakai   H. Yamashita   B. Kawamoto

Honolulu Japanese Senior Baseball league, 1939

Japanese All-Stars Are Picked

By JOHN K. FUKAO

Francis Funai's Azumas, now in the thick of the race for the championship round honors, landed the most players on the All-Star squad selected last evening for the 1940 Honolulu Japanese Senior Baseball league.

The A's were honored with four positions while the Moiliilis received three berths, the Wahiawas two and Kakaakos and Palamas one each.

Masao (Ewa) Okuda, Palamas slugger who won the individual batting championship with .611, was not only placed on the squad as utility player, but also named the most valuable player of the circuit.

The committee also named Daniel Konno, Azumas' shortstop this season, as the outstanding rookie. Konno was not placed on the All-Star team.

Here are the 1940 "stars" and their records:

	Batting	Fielding
Pitcher—Tom Kameda (Wahiawa)	.407	.947
Pitcher—Ed Kitamura (Azuma)	.071	1.000
Catcher—George Ikeno (Azuma)	.310	1.000
Firstbase—Susumu Tanaka (Azuma)	.357	.973
Secondbase—Tsuneo Omiya (Moiliili)	.203	.961
Thirdbase—Takeo Takeuchi (Moiliili)	.321	.926
Shortstop—Iwa Mamiya (Kakaako)	.350	.977
Leftfield—Tom Ige (Azuma)	.286	.941
Centerfield—Masao Nakai (Moiliili)	.385	1.000
Rightfield—Norio Matsuura (Wahiawa)	.417	1.000
Utility—Masayuki Okuda (Palama)	.611	.867

Honolulu Japanese Senior Baseball league, 1940

Okuda Is Named Most Valuable

Japanese League Selects All-Star Team — Konno, Azuma Shortstop, Adjudged Outstanding Rookie of Regular Series

The all-stars, the most valuable player, and the outstanding rookie of the Honolulu Japanese Senior Baseball league were selected last night by a special committee headed by the league manager Ralph Tempuku.

Masa (Ewa) Okuda, versatile Palama player, was voted the most valuable player. Due to his amazing hitting he was picked over Tom Kameda of Wahiawa.

Playing in six games, Okuda cracked out a brilliant .611 batting average, making 11 hits in 18 times at bat. His fielding average was .867. He batted in eight runs and tallied 11. The most versatile player in the league, he was used by Coach Wop Shinagawa in practically every position. He was used as a third baseman, second baseman, first baseman, catcher, and pitcher and he played every position well.

Konno Best Rookie

In a vote for the outstanding rookie of the regular season Daniel Saburo Konno was selected by the committee by a unanimous vote. Playing his first year in the Japanese Senior league he performed in brilliant style for ? e Azumas. Under the careful coaching of Coach Francis Funai, Konno has developed into a fine shortstop. His first year in fast competition, he hit .387, a great record. Playing in every game, he garnered 12 hits in 31 times up. His fielding average was .829. He was one of the spark plugs of the Azuma team that finished at the top of the league in the first round.

In picking the all-stars the committee went into a close huddle before starting their selections.

The pitchers were the first ones discussed and Eddie Kitamura of the Azumas and Tom Kameda of Wahiawa were chosen without opposition. Playing with the Azumas, Kitamura has come into his own. With his fine side arm hurling he pitched his team to four victories nad carried them into the championship series at the head of the circuit. He was charged with only one defeat.

The infielders chosen were Sus Tanaka of Azuma, first base; Tsune Omiya of Moiliili, second base; Iwa Mamiya of Kakaako, shortstop, and Blackie Takeuchi of Moiliili, third base.

First Round Averages of Honolulu Senior Japanese League

	G	AB	R	H	Tb	Rbi	Sb	Pct.	FA
Kawamoto (P)	6	19	8	10	14	5	1	.526	.933
M. Miike (P)	5	16	3	8	10	3	1	.500	1.000
Nakamura (S)	4	14	3	7	7	0	1	.500	.857
S. Tanaka (A)	6	21	6	10	14	6	4	.476	.981
Takata (N)	6	26	14	12	18	3	4	.462	.788
Takeuchi (M)	6	22	9	10	14	7	8	.455	.955
I. Kurata (N)	6	21	5	9	18	5	0	.429	.750
Eguchi (P)	4	12	3	5	5	8	1	.417	1.000
Uchida (W)	4	10	1	4	4	0	0	.400	1.000
J. Hironaka (N)	6	24	7	9	12	5	3	.375	.909
Yanagida (W)	6	11	3	4	4	0	0	.364	.956
Mamiya (S)	6	22	8	8	14	5	4	.364	.921
Ikegami (P)	6	11	3	4	5	2	1	.364	.333
G. Miyagawa (N)	6	17	9	6	12	5	3	.353	.929
Ige (A)	6	20	2	7	11	2	0	.350	.857
Higashi (K)	6	23	2	8	8	4	1	.348	1.000
Watanabe (P)	2	3	0	1	1	0	0	.333	1.000
Beppu (A)	5	12	3	4	4	0	0	.333	1.000
Moriguchi (P)	4	12	2	4	7	3	0	.333	1.000
Fujii (P)	6	21	9	7	8	2	5	.333	1.000
Uesugi (K)	6	21	5	7	9	4	2	.323	.985
Sadayasu (A)	2	3	0	1	1	1	1	.333	1.000
Y. Hironaka (N)	4	9	0	3	3	3	1	.333	.667
Y. Hironaka (N)	4	9	0	3	3	3	1	.333	.667
Kitaura (S)	2	6	1	2	2	1	1	.333	1.000
Kusuno (N)	6	6	1	2	2	2	0	.333	1.000
E. Suzuki (M)	2	3	0	1	1	0	0	.333	1.000
Y. Omiya (M)	6	25	4	8	10	8	1	.320	.974
Nakai (M)	6	22	8	7	15	8	5	.318	.963
Yoshida (W)	6	22	4	7	9	2	1	.318	.953
Hirasa (N)	6	22	6	7	8	0	2	.318	.923
Tomai (S)	6	23	7	7	7	1	1	.304	.935
Kirihara (K)	6	23	5	7	7	0	6	.304	.917
T. Omiya (M)	6	20	6	6	8	3	0	.300	1.000
Yamashita (S)	6	20	3	6	6	0	5	.300	.917

HONOLULU

	AB	R	BH	PO	A	E
I. Ige, lf	5	1	2	7	0	0
O. Ikeno, c	1	0	1	10	0	1
D. Kuano, ss	0	0	0	0	0	1
S. Tanaka, 1b	4	0	2	8	0	1
R. Yoshimura, 3b	4	0	2	2	1	0
O. Fujii, rf	3	0	1	0	0	0
T. Beppu, cf	3	0	0	2	0	0
D. Miura, 2b	2	0	0	1	1	0
T. Uchizaki, p	0	0	0	0	0	0
E. Suzuki, p	4	0	1	2	0	1
I. Mamiya, ss	3	0	1	0	2	0
F. Nakamura, c	3	1	1	3	1	0
T. Takeuchi, 2b	2	1	0	1	0	0
*T. Kaineda	0	0	0	0	0	0
**K. Uemai	0	0	0	0	0	0
***W. Katsunuma	0	0	0	0	0	0
Totals	34	3	9	14	6	4

*Batted for Beppu in 9th.
**Ran for Kaineda in 9th.
***Batted for Suzuki in 9th.

OAHU

	AB	R	BH	PO	A	E
T. Koike, lf	2	0	2	2	0	0
S. Hedani, rf	3	1	2	1	0	0
J. Takata, ss	4	0	2	4	1	0
H. Warashina, 2b	4	2	2	2	1	0
C. Tanaka, cf	3	1	2	7	0	0
L. Kishinami, 1b	3	0	0	6	1	0
S. Higuchi, c	4	0	1	5	2	0
T. Watanabe, 3b	4	0	2	1	2	0
H. Ohira, p	1	0	0	1	2	0
K. Kobayashi, lf, cf	1	0	0	2	0	0
M. Miyaxi, lf	0	0	0	0	0	0
C. Takata, p	3	0	0	0	1	0
Totals	31	4	9	27	15	3

Score By Innings

Honolulu .... 000 000 001—3
Oahu .... 200 001 01x—4

KAUAI

	AB	R	BH	PO	A	E
K. Hirota, rf, cf	4	0	1	1	1	0
S. Honda, c	4	0	2	4	2	1
S. Gushikuma, ss	4	1	2	5	0	1
G. Kashiwaeda, lf	3	0	2	2	0	0
J. Doi, rf	2	0	0	1	0	0
N. Mamura, 3b	4	0	1	2	3	0
J. Yamamoto, 1b	4	0	0	8	0	0
S. Matsunaga, 2b	4	0	2	1	4	2
T. Furutani, p	2	0	0	0	0	1
Sasaki, rf	2	0	0	0	1	0
F. Fujita, ss	1	0	0	0	0	1
Shimatsu, p	1	0	1	0	0	0
*Nakamoto	1	0	0	0	0	0
**L. Hirota	1	0	0	0	0	0
Totals	36	1	11	24	11	6

*Batted for Hirota in 9th.
**Batted for Honda in 9th.

OAHU

	AB	R	BH	PO	A	E
Y. Koike, lf	1	0	0	0	0	1
S. Hedani, rf	5	2	2	0	0	0
J. Takata, ss	5	1	1	1	0	1
H. Warashina, 2b	3	0	1	4	2	0
S. Higuchi, c	3	1	2	11	0	0
K. Kobayashi, cf	1	0	0	1	0	0
L. Kishinami, 1b	3	1	2	7	0	0
T. Watanabe, 3b	4	0	0	1	4	0
C. Takata, p	1	1	1	1	1	0
M. Miyazi, rf	1	0	0	1	0	0
M. Higuchi, p	3	1	1	0	3	0
L. Kunihisa, lf	2	1	0	0	0	0
C. Tanaka, cf	2	1	0	0	0	0
K. Fukuda, lf	0	0	0	0	0	0
Totals	34	7	11	27	10	2

Score By Innings

Kauai .... 000 010 000—1
Oahu .... 001 010 05x—7

HIGUCHI STARS AS OAHU STOPS URBAN CHAMPS

Sparks Spectacular Double Play in 9th to Kill Azuma Rally

Cutting off a desperate last inning rally with one of the most spectacular double plays seen at the Stadium, the Rural Oahu's Waialuas nosed out Honolulu's Azumas, 4 to 3, to set the stage for their final victory over Kauai to annex the Inter-Island championship.

Trailing 4-2 going into the 9th inning, the famous Azuma "clutch hitting," surged to the fore but Coach Francis Funai's cohorts played a long chance and lost, failing to tie the score by one run.

Waialua played magnificently in the 9th with each player handling the ball doing his chores perfectly.

Big Ed Suzuki of Moiliili gave Honolulu's waning hopes a spark of life in the 9th when he singled after Tom Kameda of Wahiawa, pinch-hitting for Tadao Beppu, was "beaned" by Charley Taketa and Takeo Takeuchi of Moiliili had forced out Ken Hamai, pinch-running for Tom.

Takeuch went to second on Suzuki's hit. Katsunuma replaced Suzuki as pinch-runner. Tom Ige, who covered his left field territory brilliantly, singled sharply to center field. Kichi Kobayashi, coming in for the ball, allowed it to roll past him and Takeuchi scored.

Quick Recovery

Katsunuma rounded third and scampered for home with what would have been the tying run. Left Fielder Miyagi, however, covered Kobayashi and scooped up the ball, whipping it to Shortstop Joe

"Waialuas nosed out Honolulu's Azumas, 4 to 3 . . ."

KEIO

	AB	R	H	PO	A	E
Miyazaki, 2b						
Meru, lf						
Nakata, cf						
Odachi, ss						
Inouye, c						
Kusumoto, rf						
Iwamoto, 1b						
Narita, p						
Nagara, 2b						
Takatsuka, p						
Uno, 3b						
Totals	31			27		

ASAHI

	AB	R	H	PO	A	E
Takata, 2b						
Yoshimura, 2b						
Kunihisa, ss-3b						
Ireno, c						
Ohta, 1b						
M. Fujii, rf						
Igo, cf						
Kawamoto, lf						
Suzuki, p						
Moriguchi, p						
Yoda, ss						
Nakajo, c						
O. Fujii, lf						
Takuma, 3b						
Tanaka						
Fujishige						
Totals				27		

Keio University box scores

against Keio University of the Tokyo Big Six college baseball league. Ever since I was in grade school, teams from the Tokyo Big Six—usually Meij, Waseda, or Keio—came for a series of games with Hawaii League teams at the Honolulu Stadium. We all followed these games very closely, and my dad always used to promise to take us to some of these games if we worked very hard on the farm during the summer. This was the high point of the summer for us. Never in my wildest dreams did I imagine myself in an Asahi uniform playing against Keio University. I know my dad was most happy and proud of me (see box score).

I'd like to add one more fact to my Asahi experience. Unknown to most baseball fans, I was the first, perhaps the only, player of Okinawan descent to play for Asahi before World War II. Wally Yomamine, Masa Yonamine, Shin Yogi, and others—far better players than I was—emerged, but this was primarily in the post-war period. I was reminded of this fact by many of my fellow Okinawans and urged by them to do my best.

Chinese Land Four On Hawaii Loop All-Stars

By LOUI LEONG HOP

As a dying kick to the local baseball campaign and to furnish ammunition for a blitzkrieg at the direction of our noggin this scribe is today naming his 1940 Hawaii (senior) league all-star team and teams.

Besides picking the first and second combinations (many will say there won't be much difference in either outfit anyway) this scrivener has also selected an All-Rookie lineup.

Before going any further we wish to state that the players selected are for the entire season and not for performances in the regular series, the Cartwright tournament or in the interisland games in which only the championship winning All-Chinese participated.

The value of a player to his team is placed ahead of hitting and fielding averages. Consistency and popularity with the fans are other factors for our final selections.

On our first team the title grabbing Chinese won four positions, the Wanderers five and the Braves and Asahis one each.

The Hawaiians and Navy, who were eliminated from the Cartwright series, failed to get a man on the first team.

The Second Team

The second string saw the Wanderers and Chinese getting four each while the Navy, Hawaiians and Braves one apiece. The Asahis were not able to crash into this lineup.

The Asahis, however, landed the most on the All-Rookie outfit with four, followed by the Braves with three, the Chinese two and the Hawaiians and Wanderers one apiece.

Below is how the teams look to us:

FIRST TEAM

Pos. Player	Team
C—Henry Wong	Chinese
P—K. Cruickshank	Wanderers
P—Eddie Kaulukukui	Chinese
1B—Pat Gleason	Wanderers
2B—Joe Rose	Wanderers
3B—Ray Victor	Chinese
SS—Tom Kaulukukui	Chinese
LF—Hans Pung	Wanderers
CF—Johnny Kerr	Wanderers
RF—George Indie	Braves
U—Lawrence Kunihisa	Asahis

SECOND TEAM

Pos. Player	Team
C—L. Atkinson	Wanderers
P—Al Nalua	Hawaiians
P—Ted Shaw	Chinese
1B—John Samia	Chinese
2B—Ed Farm	Chinese
3B—D. K. Richards	Wanderers
SS—Manuel Ferreira	Braves
LF—Masao Nakai	Wanderers
CF—Joseph Awa	Chinese
RF—Ken Ward	Navy
U—Maynard Piltz	Wanderers

ROOKIE TEAM

Pos. Player	Team
C—George Ikeno	Asahis
P—L. Kasparovitch	Braves
P—Herb Spinola	Braves
1B—Benny Wong	Chinese
2B—Tsuneo Omiya	Asahis
3B—Valentine Wong	Chinese
SS—Ernest Neves	Braves
LF—Hideo Yamashita	Asahis
CF—Tom Ige	Asahis
RF—Roy Banks	Wanderers
U—Andrew Farley	Hawaiians

We could write columns for the why and wherefores of our selections but lacking the space we'll let the above lineups explain themselves.

One other factor that influenced our choices a lot was that in a tight fight the player with the championship winning team got the nod.

It has been a most successful season, from all reports. Two teams made trips away, the Asahis to Japan and the Wanderers to Cuba, and Keio university of Japan "invaded" the islands.

Despite the heavy schedule, including the interisland frays, the senior league came out in the clear financially in all projects with the exception, of course, of the Havana tournament which is the question mark.

I did make the Rookie All-Star Team, 1940

Baseball at University of Hawaii
1937–1940, 1954

Baseball was always a big part of sports at the University. In the early thirties the team toured Japan and Manchuria under Coach "Proc" Klum. In the late thirties we played in the A.S.U.H. League and later in the Hawaii Junior League. The latter was the "farm" league for the senior Hawaii League teams; Asahi, Braves, Wanderers, Chinese, Hawaiians, with the addition of one team from the Filipino community.

We had some players of Hawaii League caliber at the University—the Kaulukukui brothers, Tommy and Joe, Calton Loo of the Chinese, Sus Tanaka of Asahi, and Ezra Wolfe and James Carey of the Wanderers. Since our league played before the start of the senior league, it was possible and permissible to play in both leagues. The Kaulukukui boys were big stars in all sports at the University and it was a great pleasure to play with them. In some games I caught for Joe and in others I had Tommy catch for me. Since the league itself was second rate, not too much attention was given to it.

We made one trip to Maui for a series of games. This was especially good for the Maui boys on our team—Tadao Beppu, Mike Kinoshita, and Angel Maehara. The highlight of this trip was playing against Kahului and Puunene at a festival in up-country Ulupolukoa on the slope of Mt. Haleakala.

My last personal involvement with baseball came thirteen years later, after my return from the war and graduate work—this time not as a player but as a coach of the University of Hawaii team in 1954. Hank Vasconcellos, then Athletic Director at the University, had just elevated the baseball program by entering us for the first time into the Hawaii League. Throughout the year I received generous volunteer help from knowledgeable baseball veterans Charles Souza of the Braves, Iwa Mamiya of Asahi, and my old buddy, Tadao Beppu. Vasconcellos paid me the handsome sum of $300 for the entire season. Actually, he gave me the job because he couldn't get anyone else. Jimmy Asato, who had coached the team the year before, gave up in disgust. The last straw, he told me, was losing a game at the old Moiliili field when the opponents' fly-ball to left field got caught in the big tree.

The Hawaii Baseball League, which was then the top league in the territory, always played their games at the Honolulu Stadium where fans had to pay admission to see the games. The players I inherited were barely above the high school level of play. Going against seasoned players such as the Braves, Asahi, and the Wanderers was more than a match for our young players. Less than half a dozen of my boys would have been able to make Coach Les Murakami's University of Hawaii team of the 1980s. Only two of my players had previous experience in the Hawaii League—Stan Hashimoto with the Rural Red Sox and Mitch Shishido with Asahi. Other players with good high school credentials, however, performed creditably. Despite our poor record, I remain proud of the boys I led. I must add that their performances after graduation in the various prestigious positions they held, and still hold, in the state also made me proud. I don't recall a single academic problem on the team with only four or five boys on "tuition only" scholarships. We recruited no out-of-state players; we had no funds to do so.

We had no stadium of our own. The lower campus was referred to as the quarry and our baseball field was in a slightly improved section, with a backstop and skinned diamond to distinguish it from the rest of the quarry. No league games were actually played here, but we sometimes held practice games. There was one game here I can never forget. It was a practice game against the Kaneohe Marines. Playing third base for me was a spark plug from Maui named Alfred DeLoso. Coaching at third base for the marines was their coach, a major. With no forewarning, my third baseman began to charge the marine coach who was a good hundred pounds bigger than my man. DeLoso was yelling at the coach, "You can't call us gooks." After a small brawl, I was able to help stabilize the situation when my catcher, Byson Jung, yelled, "Ye, DeLoso, he called you a gook." The fight started all over again, but, in the end, better heads prevailed.

Since I already had a full teaching load, I couldn't spend the time necessary to develop the team, so after one year, I threw

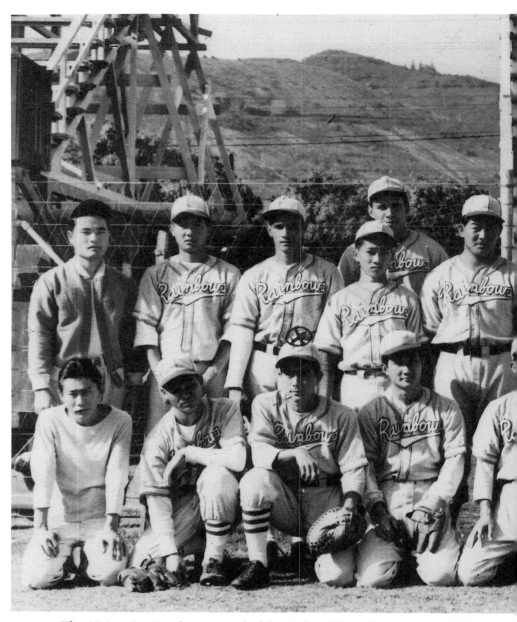

The University Rainbows, coached by Luke Gill, will open the ASUH League season this afternoon with a game against the Chinese. *Left to right, front row:* S. Toda, T. Ogawa, T. Ige, T. Uchigaki, H. Murashige, H. Hiroki, T. Yamahira, F. Miike, Y. Yasui. *Second row:* T. Beppu, S. Saiki,

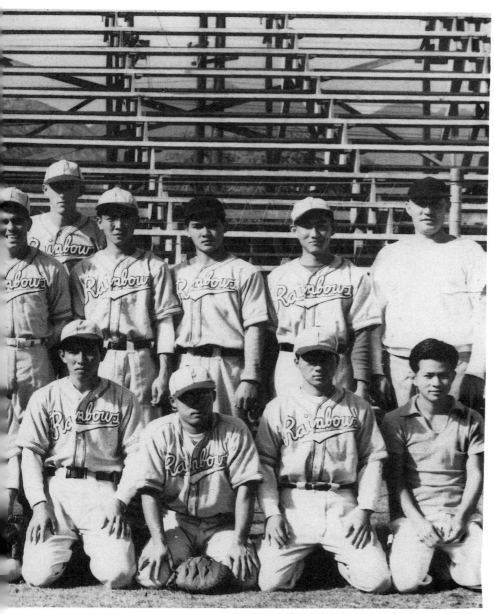

J. Kaulukukui, M. Katagiri, S. Tanaka, James Carey, T. Nishizaki, S. Maehara, M. Kinoshita, captain; Luke Gill, coach. *Third row:* M. Desha,
E. Wolff. (*Honolulu Advertiser* photo)

UH Tossers Turn Back All-Filipinos

Ige Pitches Great Ball, Allowing Fils Only 4 Bingles

The University of Hawaii tossers took the All-Filipinos into camp yesterday in a Hawaii junior league game, 5-1. Coach Luke Gill started Thomas Ige on the mound, who pitched superbly. Aided by almost flawless support Ige fanned three batters and allowed only four hits. His opponent, Mancao, also hurled steady ball but bunched hits spelled his ruin. He fanned six Deans.

The Rainbow lads crossed the plate first when Miike singled sharply to centerfield. Tanaka hit a weird triple to push over the former. In the fourth stanza, Tanaka, first batter up, hit a long homer to centerfield. Another run was chalked up in the fifth when, after having stolen second, Johnson came in on Katagiri's smashing single through the keystone sack. Tommy Kaulukukui, who performed well behind the plate, hit a circuit clout in the eighth canto, sending Tanaka home ahead of him. The Deahsmen were never headed throughout the whole game. But for a fumbled grounder by T. Ogawa, the Varsity men played fine ball. Tanaka, Tommie Kaulukukui, and Katagiri each got two hits.

The All-Filipinos were held back by only four measly hits, one of them good for a round tripper, hit by C. Barcenilla in the last chapter. Nifty playing by the Rainbow infield men killed all of the Filipinos' chances to score. By winning the University of Hawaii are sole leaders of the Hawaii Junior Baseball league, with three wins and no dosses.

A large crowd of over one thousand plantation folks witnessed the game which was played at the Oahu Sugar Baseball diamond.

Fair weather permitting, there will be two games at John Wise Field tomorrow. At 9 a. m. the Asahis and the Wanderers will tangle, while in the second game, the All-Chinese and All-Hawaiians will fight it out to get out of the cellar.

All-Filipinos

	AB	R	BH	PO	A	E
J. Estrera, 2b	2	0	0	2	1	0
F. Paculba, rf	2	0	0	0	0	0
F. Barcenilla, 3b	4	0	0	1	3	0
J. Primasio, ss	2	0	0	0	1	0
A. Enanoria, 1b	3	0	1	6	0	0
C. Mancao, p	3	0	0	1	1	0
B. Barcenilla, lf	2	0	1	3	0	0
A. Rania, cf	3	0	0	2	0	0
H. Barcelona, c	2	0	1	4	0	0
Lee Lleces, 2b	1	0	0	0	0	1
C. Barcenilla, rf	1	1	1	1	0	0
F. Daguman, ss	2	0	0	2	0	0
Lunasco, c	1	0	0	2	0	0
Totals	28	1	4	24	6	1

Uni. of Hawaii

	AB	R	BH	PO	A	E
M. Katagiri, ss	4	0	2	2	2	0
Miike, 3b	3	1	1	1	2	0
Ogawa, 2b	4	0	0	3	4	1
Tanaka, 1b	2	2	2	10	0	0
T. Kaulukukui, c	4	1	2	5	1	0
Saiki, cf	4	0	0	3	0	0
Young, lf	2	0	0	1	0	0
Johnson, rf	3	1	1	0	0	0
Ige, p	3	0	0	1	2	0
Kinoshita, lf	1	0	0	0	0	0
Beppu, rf	1	0	0	1	0	0
Totals	31	5	8	27	11	1

"In some games I caught for Joe and in others I had Tommy catch for me." *Honolulu Advertiser,* April 1938

Shown above is the board of strategy for the University of Hawaii 1954 baseball team. Stan Hashimoto (left), captain of the team is shown talking it over with Dr. Thomas Ige, manager of the team. (Johnny Uyehara photo)

UNIVERSITY OF HAWAII	AB	R	H	PO	A	E
R. Omuro, cf	3	0	0	2	0	0
A. Deloso, 3b	4	0	1	0	1	0
D. Agcaoili, lf rf (7)	0	1	0	1	1	0
S. Hashimoto, 1b	3	2	2	7	0	0
A. Tarumoto, 2b	4	0	2	4	3	0
Y. Asato, rf	2	0	0	4	0	0
R. Koike, c	4	0	0	7	1	0
M. Shishido, ss	2	0	0	1	2	0
T. Kinoshita, p	3	0	0	2	1	0
T. Odo, lf, ss (L6)	2	1	1	0	0	0
K. Teragawachi, rf (7)	2	0	2	1	0	0
K. Izutani, p (6)	1	0	0	0	0	0
a-J. Nakamura pr (6)	0	0	0	0	0	0
Y. Kakazu lf (9)	0	0	0	1	0	0
b-E. Usui pr (8)	0	1	0	0	0	0
G. Serikaku p, (8)	1	0	1	0	0	0
TOTALS	36	5	9	37	10	0

a—Ran for Izutani.
b—Ran for Kinoshita.

BRAVES	AB	R	H	PO	A	E
J. Wann, 2b	3	1	1	5	5	0
J. Ayres, 3b	3	0	1	2	5	0
Joe Tom, ss	3	0	2	5	0	4
W. Kaneko, 1b	2	1	1	7	0	0
B. Azevedo, rf	4	0	2	0	0	0
J. Gomard, lf	4	0	0	3	0	0
H. Neves, cf	4	0	1	2	0	0
W. Cummings, c	4	0	1	1	0	1
Chris Mancao, p	1	0	0	0	2	0
x-S. Neves, ph (9)	1	0	0	0	0	0
TOTALS	31	3	9	27	12	5

x—forced Cummings for Mancao.

Runs by Innings
U. of Hawaii .... 010 000 060—5
Braves .... 000 110 000—3

in the towel. Upon retiring I recommended Toku Tanaka to succeed me. He was a big star with "Peanut" Kunishisa's Rural Red Sox, which dominated the Hawaii League for many years. With Toku, the University of Hawaii team became more respectable and gradually became competitive. Some of his players moved into other Hawaii Senior League teams after playing for the University. They were Allen Yamamoto, George Anzai, Lefty Hirano, George Surikaku, John Nakamura, Ken Nakakura, Lefty Matsuwaka, and others.

CHAPTER 4

Off to the Mainland
1941–1953

To do graduate work on the mainland during the depression of the thirties was, or should have been, one of those major decisions of a lifetime. I must candidly admit that in my case it was more a spur of the moment decision. Several factors, however, led me to make this decision. First, and foremost, I felt I was getting nowhere with my job with the Matson Navigation Company and future prospects there looked very dim indeed. My job on the waterfront involved clerking, checking freight coming in and seeing that it was dispatched to the proper consignees. My job became very routine, and checking labels in the semi-darkness of the enclosed piers was damaging to my eyes. I needed a change.

It didn't take much to quit, although it was considered quite a good job in job-scarce Honolulu. The last straw happened on the day I saw my long-time buddy from high school and the University, Harry Oshima, leave for New York on the Matson liner *Lurline* to do graduate work at Columbia. I decided almost at that moment that I too would leave for graduate school. When I finally left in February of 1941, about six months after my friend departed, I was very confused and had only a faint idea what I was to study. I had not even been accepted by any graduate school and had very little money to back up my new and daring venture. Although my family on our little taro farm in Kahaluu was very supportive, they were in no position to help me financially. Without any savings of my own, with parents too poor to help out, I was very determined but utterly frustrated.

My financial dilemma was initially solved by a five-hun-

OFF TO MAINLAND: Tom Ige (above) left
for the mainland at noon today. A graduate
of the local university where he starred in
baseball, Tommy will attend the University of Chicago for a special business course.
He also played with the champion Azumas
in the Honolulu Japanese Senior league.

dred dollar loan from Mr. George Higa, who owned the Honolulu Cafe at the corner of Beretania and Fort Streets. He knew
me only as a member of the Japanese Senior League Azuma
baseball team. The Azuma team had had "Honolulu Cafe"
advertised on the backs of our baseball uniforms. Mr. Higa
was a most generous friend and helped me without questions
regarding my plans or how I was going to pay back his loan. It
was thirteen years later on my return to Hawaii that I finally
repaid him.

His help was very decisive in getting me started and I have
been forever grateful. In retrospect, I believe the reason he

supported me was to advance the career of a fellow Okinawan. It has been generally observed that Okinawans in Hawaii have helped each other. In this case, I was the beneficiary. Much later I tried to help him when he was faced with bankruptcy in the sixties.

Chicago—1940

In Chicago I was very fortunate again in getting the help of Dr. Herbert Bloomer, then professor of sociology at the University of Chicago and also the editor of the prestigious *American Journal of Sociology*. I had gotten to know Dr. Bloomer when he was on leave and taught at the University of Hawaii in 1939. He was an outstanding scholar and very impressive in other ways too. He was an all-American football lineman at the University of Kansas and he played professional football for the Chicago Bears in the late twenties. At 6'8" he was one of the "Monsters from the Midway." While at the University of Hawaii, he showed interest in our sports programs. He helped out with our football program, and I attended several social affairs of our "H" club with him. With his help, I had no problem being admitted into the graduate economics program. I found out, though, that the University of Chicago, unlike other prestigious schools, was very easy to get into but very difficult to get out of. Most graduate students never completed their degrees because the standards were so high.

My major professor in the graduate school was Dr. Paul H. Douglas. I was introduced to him by our mutual friend, Dr. Bloomer. Dr. Douglas was one of the leading scholars in the nation in the field of social legislation. He made his reputation during the twenties in child labor and minimum wage-hour laws. In addition to being an outstanding scholar, he was an extremely colorful individual. He became and remained my idol and role model throughout my life. At the time I was taking his courses, during the spring and summer terms of 1941, he was also a city councilman. He was an outspoken critic of corruption and waste in Chicago and occasionally made headlines. I remember one speech he made to a Presby-

terian ministers' conference at the University. When asked
how he managed to survive in the rough and tumble politics
of Chicago, especially in light of his severe challenge to the
powerful mobs, he claimed he had absolutely no fear in tack-
ling the mobsters. He said the code of the underworld was
superior to that of the upperworld. As long as you didn't enter
into any agreement with the mobs and later betray them, you
had absolutely no fear of retaliation. He said he could trust
the code of the underworld more than that of the upperworld.
Despite his unorthodox modus operandi, he was very popular
and was easily elected to the U.S. Senate after the war.

While attending the University of Chicago, I lived initially
at the International House, also known as the "I House,"
adjoining the campus. It was built and supported by the Rockefeller Foundation (similiar to the one at Columbia University). Many of the students from Hawaii lived at the "I
House" or gathered with friends there, among them Abraham
Akaka, Seido Ogawa, Mits Aoki, and Toshimi Tatsuyama,
who was preparing for the ministry. Tets Watanabe was in the
medical school; Iwalani Smith, along with many girls, was
studying social work. We got together often to eat chop suey
whenever we got homesick.

After a few months, I began to realize that being friendly
only with Hawaiians was not very helpful in getting to know
other students, and so I moved to a student co-op across Stagg
Field.

While I was attending the University of Chicago, the German forces were devastating western Europe, and England
was under heavy attack. In our country there was a sharp division between those who thought we should enter the war on
the side of Great Britain and France and the isolationists, who
argued that we should stay out of "their war." President
Roosevelt repeated again and again that American boys would
not be sent to fight on foreign soil—but that we were indirectly aiding the allies with supplies, as well as escorting
ships carrying war materials to Britain.

The *Chicago Tribune*, which called itself the "greatest
newspaper in America," was leading the America First movement to keep America out of the conflict. Robert Hutchins,

then president of the University of Chicago, in a speech delivered at the Rockefeller Church on the campus, strongly favored non-involvement. This speech influenced me more than anything else for I had a very high regard for President Hutchins.

There was one experience on the eve of our entry in World War II that I vividly remember. During the summer of 1941, while attending classes at the University of Chicago, I usually spent the late afternoons running around the track at the Amos Alonzo Stagg Stadium on the campus. The exercise usually ended with me climbing the bleachers and sunning myself. I was greatly shocked to learn much later that the vital atomic bomb experiments of Enrico Fermi and associates were being conducted in the bleachers right below me! This was during the period when all Japanese were being restricted from sensitive West Coast areas, and there I was literally sitting right above probably the most secretive wartime activity. Nobody ever questioned my presence there, however.

That same summer, I, Wing Kong Chong, Harry Oshima, and others from Columbia University made a tour of the mid-Atlantic states in one car. This was my first trip south of the Mason-Dixon line, and I was incensed with the "Black" and "White" designations on various facilities. We generally entered the facilities reserved for "White" persons and were never challenged. While traveling through Virginia, we stopped at the University of Virginia in Charlottesville to hear a lecture by Major George Fielding Elliot, who was probably the leading expert on military-related matters at that time. Hitler had just begun his surprise invasion into Russia, which added a completely new dimension to the war in Europe. In his speech Major Elliot claimed that Hitler would subdue the Russians in three to four months. As erroneous as this turned out to be, I believe most of our military observers shared his view at that time.

Professor Douglas left the University of Chicago after the summer session of 1941. Although a Quaker and pacifist, he volunteered for the U.S. Marines. As he was then over fifty years of age, an exception had to be made to permit him to join the service. Although he was big and husky, having played football at Columbia during his college days, going in as a private with white hair attracted much publicity in Chicago during that summer. Assigned to headquarter duties with the 6th Division of the Marine Corps, he went through the bitter battles throughout the South Pacific. Stories appeared in the media about his joining the front-line fighting when the battle got too intense for him to remain at headquarters. He was reputed to be very adept at using a flame thrower to rout out the enemy from caves.

During the battle of Okinawa, I learned that Douglas was also there with the 6th Division Marines. By then, he was a major. I tried on several occasions to locate him, but before I could find him, he was evacuated because of a serious wound in his right hand. He carried a badly withered right arm with him for the rest of his life.

University of Wisconsin—1941

When Professor Douglas, my major professor, left the University of Chicago, I transferred to the University of Wisconsin in the fall of 1941. This was a big shift for me in terms of academic emphasis. The Chicago school of economics was widely regarded as right wing, with leaders like professors Frank Knight, Henry Simons, Gregg Lewis, and later Milton Friedman. Douglas was the only noted "liberal" on the staff. The Wisconsin school of economics was almost at the other extreme. It wasn't left wing in a political or economic sense, but basically it was action-oriented, in contrast to the theoretical bent of Chicago economists. In Wisconsin, in close collaboration with the state legislature, they were pioneering legislation in workmen's compensation, wage house laws, state income tax, and public utilities. Wisconsin was the home base for the Lafollette brothers and the Progressive Party. Professor John R. Commons, Selig Perlman, Edwin Witte, Harold Groves, and Martin Glaeser led the "activist" economics. Dr. Walter Heller was an outstanding example of a Wisconsin alumnus. Upon meeting Heller for the first time, President Kennedy was impressed with his pragmatic approach. Kennedy later appointed him to head his economic council. Heller also helped structure the economy of war-torn Germany immediately after World War II and continued to guide the American economy under presidents Lyndon Johnson and Jimmy Carter. Given all of these factors, I felt more at home at Wisconsin than at Chicago.

December 7, 1941

When war broke out on December 7, 1941, I was at a chop suey house in downtown Madison with an old high school and University of Hawaii friend, Ben Takayesu. Ben was in the law school then. After I got home, he called me with the big news.

Ben immediately quit school and joined the U.S. Army. I tried to enlist in the navy but was refused. The air force refused me too. I decided to wait. However, a few days later, I did report to the FBI office in Madison to let them know of my presence and what I was doing there. I had no further contact with them after that, but I felt a lot better.

I received a scholarship in 1942 as research assistant to Professor Martin Glaeser, nationally known in the field of public utilities and also known as editor of *Land Economics*. Public utilities was not my major field of interest, and I was surprised to get this much-needed financial help. I worked with Professor Glaeser on the Tennessee Valley Authority (TVA) projects and on his special interest project—the Los Angeles Water System. In retrospect, I sometimes shudder at the thought that I was working on all the intricate details of the vast and vital system of water flows throughout southern California. The FBI might have been able to work up a good case of potential sabotage against me, even stronger than that of most of the Niseis evacuated from the West Coast. Nothing ever happened and I am grateful.

I have often wondered why Professor Glaeser chose me to assist him, as I had practically no knowledge in his field. I am inclined to believe he felt sorry for me in my plight and wanted to help me. He was of German descent and told me of the many hardships his whole family suffered during the First World War in rural Wisconsin. I'm sure he wanted to spare me some of the same heartache. Later I named my son after him. He visited my family in Hawaii in 1948.

About this time, in July 1942, an article appeared in *The Nation* magazine strongly advocating the evacuation of all Japanese-Americans in Hawaii in the same manner as those on the West Coast. It was written by Albert Horlings, one-time journalism professor at the University of Hawaii. He contended that Japanese in Hawaii could not be trusted and the defense of the Pacific was, therefore, exposed to grave dangers. I felt an urgency to reply immediately to this article. I knew censorship was widely imposed in Hawaii and that it would be difficult for anyone in Hawaii to reply to this article. My personal letters from Hawaii had all been censored. There was no censorship in Madison, Wisconsin, however. What follows is the entire Horlings article and my reply, which was published a few weeks later in the same magazine.

HAWAII'S 150,000 JAPANESE

BY

ALBERT HORLINGS

The United States is making one of the most dramatic bets of history in Hawaii. It is gambling the internal stability of its greatest base in the Pacific— the anchor of the whole Pacific battleline—on the loyalty of 150,000 Japanese and Japanese Americans, 40,000 of whom are aliens, the majority of whom cannot read or speak English, and few of whom have ever seen America or have a clear understanding of what America stands for.

This is no mean wager. A Japanese fifth column in Hawaii could do great damage during an attempted invasion. It could halt civilian transportation, block highways, destroy vulnerable reservoirs upon which Honolulu depends for water, wreck gas and electric service, destroy food, and terrorize civilians. By

diverting manpower for the exterior defenses this
fifth column could turn defeat for the invader into
success. Sabotage would be easy for it; the Japanese
population is 40 percent of the total and its members
hold hundreds of strategic positions in public utilities, in civilian defense, and in other services.

We might deserve praise for risking so much on
the human heart if only we were not making the bet
for the wrong reasons. I suspect we are making it not
because the military authorities in Hawaii really
trust the Japanese but because pressure has been
brought on them, and they have been told that the
economic life of the islands will collapse without
the Japanese. Hawaiian business men are variously
motivated, but some of them appear to favor a liberal policy toward the Japanese simply because they
favor business as usual. And in the background hov-
ers the case for Hawaiian statehood. The Japanese
in Hawaii have long been held up to the mainland
as first-class Americans by those pressing for the
island's admission to the Union, and many islanders
fear that to cast doubt on Japanese loyalty now
would ruin the chances of admission. The real con-
viction of the white islanders is shown by the large-
scale evacuation of women and children that has
been going on ever since Pearl Harbor.

In this historic gamble we have certainly something to win. First, we can win the confidence of
some good citizens of ours. Japanese communities
in this country have in general realized that their
members could never blend physically into the
American stream, and so far they have shown no
evidence of wanting to be anything but a Japanese
colony abroad. But a few individuals in these communities in Hawaii and in the states, have become
truly Americanized in spirit, and it would be a tragedy if they were discriminated against by measures
aimed at Japanese who merely live here. No one who
knows the able, spirited and likable American of

Japanese ancestry will underestimate the contribution these people can make to American life once they choose—and once we permit them—to turn irrevocably to the West.

We gain something by admitting that Hawaii has handled its peculiar racial problem sensibly and well, and by refusing unnecessarily to disturb the islands' equilibrium. Sociologically and genetically we have everything to win. Hawaii is one of the great anthropological laboratories of the world, and it would be easy to arouse antipathies that would destroy its value. The racial *aloha* of the islands is a real and priceless thing.

But the greatest thing we stand to gain is the aid of hundreds of millions of people whose skins are not the color of ours. Whether we win or lose the peace will probably depend greatly upon our success in convincing Asiatics, Indians, Negroes, and others that our plea for world leadership is not a screen for world domination. We must convince them that we are fighting not for an Anglo-Saxon world or a Caucasian world, but for a world in which humanity is the test of franchise.

However, our kindness to enemy aliens and enemy sympathizers at a naval outpost will avail us little so long as we needlessly affront our friends. The propaganda value of extraordinary solicitude for Hawaii's Japanese—and it is certainly extraordinary measured by Japanese and German standards, as well as by our own past performance—will be completely nullified unless we mend our manners. A Chinese seaman who was on our side years before the State Department knew which was our side is prohibited from coming ashore at an American port. And if it is true that an exclusion law aimed at all Orientals arouses more resentment than good treatment of enemy-alien Orientals can ever undo, then we must wonder whether we have not put the Honolulu cart before the Washington horse.

In any case Hawaii's safety is not a local matter, and a decision relating to control of a possible fifth column must be determined by national interests. How does our present policy look from that point of view? I am afraid it looks crazy. I never found anyone in Honolulu, not even the most enthusiastic member of the Japanese Chamber of Commerce, who would say that Hawaii's Japanese were overwhelmingly loyal to the United States. Why should they be, and why would they want us to win this war?

The political and economic fortunes of a few depend upon our winning. Some have been released from stark poverty by living under the American flag. Some had washed away the stain of ostracism that attached to their family in Japan. Some believe that America's accent upon the worth of an individual will lead to greater happiness for themselves and the world. A few would rather see a defeated Japan than a militaristic one. Some have deeply rooted prejudices and sentiments binding them to our side.

But the proportion of these is not large. The majority have nothing to gain by the defeat of Japan. Their prestige as expatriates depends in large part upon the prestige of the Japanese empire. Their economic fortunes are often tied more closely to Japan than to America: they work for Tokyo banks and business houses; they import goods from Japan; they invest in Japanese securities. Even if they live entirely off Hawaii land or its surrounding waters, their customers are likely to be members of their own race. When they work for the white man, it is in a menial position, one that is more likely to arouse resentment than regard. To a remarkable degree Hawaii's Japanese are untouched by American ways; all their pride of race, family, and religion binds them to Japan. Thousands see or hear almost nothing American, while they consume Japanese food, Japanese clothing, Japanese music, Japanese pictures, Japanese newspapers and magazines by the shipload.

In common with all the other races there, the Japanese love their purple islands, but they can imagine Hawaii without American rule. Indeed, Japanese propaganda has frequently drawn the picture of them. Instead of doing menial labor at the low end of a double wage standard, they would occupy lofty positions in the economic life of the islands. Instead of being crowded in slums, they would live in the cool valleys back of the city, from which deed restrictions now generally exclude them. Instead of seeing their children admitted to the best schools only in token numbers, they would enjoy all the emoluments of the ruling class. In hundreds of ways even the "good" Japanese would gain, not lose, by Japanese rule in Hawaii.

Nor are they unaware of these facts. In impressive numbers they fail to burn their bridges to Japan. Despite numerous campaigns for renunciation of Japanese allegiance, there are still 60,000 dual citizens in Hawaii—in other words, the majority of American-born Japanese in Hawaii are willing to let the Japanese government claim them as its own. Some 15,000 Hawaiian-born Japanese have cast their lot permanently with Japan. Thousands of others shuttle between Tokyo and Honolulu, "taking my father's ashes to his home-land," seeking better jobs, or simply taking advantage of the low steamship rates through which Japan keeps in touch with its foreign colonies.

Only a Pollyanna could conclude that there is no danger in this situation. If only because it hides the emperor's agents, this large unassimilated group constitutes a real menace. Nor are the professional saboteurs who escape the FBI the only ones who would act with zest if they found themselves in a position to swing the balance against the United States forces. There are also congenital white-man

haters (*haole*-haters in the island vernacular) among
both the alien and citizen Japanese. The most innoc-
uous *papa-san* could easily become their dupe. I do
not say he will; the point is that we cannot be sure
he will not. With no better material the emperor's
men certainly welded efficient fifth columns in
the Philippines, in Malaya, and in the Dutch East
Indies. (There is another side to the coin, and in a
happier time I would rather be polishing it—it
presents the Hawaiianization of Japanese who can
never be Americanized, for instance, and the human
qualities which we must admire in these fine people
whether they happen to be on our side or not.)

People who have been interned do not buy theater
tickets or serve cocktails, and some islanders have
argued that this is not the time to disturb matters in
civilian Honolulu. Hawaii's Congressional delegate,
Sam King, has worked assiduously to convince both
Congress and the military that nothing should be
done beyond apprehending known spies and treach-
erous ringleaders. Everywhere one hears repeated
the testimony of Captain John Anthony Burns of
the Honolulu Police force that he has found the accounts of sniping at American soldiers untrue, and
the touching story of Yoshio Yamamoto, who saves
all his pennies for war stamps. Everywhere people
emphasize that the Japanese are indispensable in
Hawaii. But many of these are interested persons
who overlook the Buddhist temples, the Japanese-
language schools, the dozens of Japanese societies
and organizations, some with official Tokyo connections, the ubiquitous pictures of the emperor, Japanese holidays, the crowds flocking to see the emper-
or's cruisers, the subscriptions to Japanese war
loans, the strongly nationalistic propaganda uncov-
ered in Japanese-language publications.

The argument of the Japanese indispensability,
the one that has been dinned into the ears Congress
and the military authorities, is a fallacious one. It

would be inconvenient to get along without the Japanese, but it would not be impossible. The Filipino has long been the backbone of the plantation labor supply, and there are thousands of Chinese, Hawaiians, Koreans, Puerto Ricans, and Caucasians to carry on essential functions. If the plantations should stop raising sugar and pineapples, which they would be forced to do during a long siege, there would be an oversupply of labor. Conversion to food crops has not taken place in Hawaii to the extent always thought necessary.

One articulate group in Hawaii advocates internment of the Japanese. The leaders of the group are life-long islanders, some of whom were raised with the Japanese and speak their language. Those I know are not given to jitters, and when they say that the absence of sabotage on December 7 proves nothing, I agree with them. If Japan has a well-organized fifth column in Hawaii it would certainly not have exposed it prematurely, before any effort was to be made at invasion, and when the saboteurs could have accomplished nothing but their own extinction.

I cannot agree, however, that large-scale internment of Hawaii's Japanese would be wise. Not only would internment be sure to cause great hardship, but it would be ineffective, in particular, in getting out of the invader's reach a large and competent reservoir of manpower which could be depended on to carry on civilian life in the islands. For whatever doubt there may be about the attitude of the Japanese before or during an invasion attempt, there is no doubt that the vast majority of Hawaii's Japanese will work with alacrity with the emperor's forces if Japan takes the islands. I favor evacuation, which would remove this labor force, bring less hardship, and reduce Hawaii's consumption of food, much of which is convoyed from California. Since ships return from Hawaii with only sugar and pineapples, which we can forego momentarily, plenty of bottoms are available for the purpose.

We should not underestimate the importance of what we are gambling. Hawaii consists of seven islands—only one of them fortified—as against the 2,500 islands of Micronesia; it is virtually our only neutralizing agent for the vast insular system of "stationary aircraft carriers" that projects Japan power south to the Equator and east to within bombing distance of Honolulu. Hawaii is indispensable to us if we are to protect our flanks in the Antipodes and Alaska, safeguard the Panama Canal and our West Coast, and eventually carry out a frontal attack on Japan. Without it we should be impotent in the Pacific.

If it was expedient to remove a scattering of Japanese from our Western coastal regions, the American people should be told why it is not many times more necessary to remove this heavier concentration of Japanese from islands which are in greater danger and harder to defend. We are playing for the highest stakes: Congress should investigate immediately and tell us what the odds are.

HAWAII'S LOYAL JAPANESE

BY

THOMAS H. IGE

In *The Nation*, August 8, 1942, p. 120, Reprinted
by permission of The Nation Co.

In his *The Nation* article of July 25, Albert Horlings scores the United States for its liberal or lax treatment of persons of Japanese extraction now residing in Hawaii. He argues that the great majority of them cannot be trusted; that we are taking a bad risk. The charges made by Mr. Horlings against these 150,000 Japanese, 110,000 of whom are American citizens, are numerous and serious. I wholly agree with Mr. Horlings that "Hawaii's safety is not a local matter, and a decision relating to a control of a possible fifth column must be determined by national interest." It does not follow, however, that a prejudiced, ill-considered presentation of the case will be any help in clarifying the situation. Being of Japanese descent, born and reared in Hawaii, I too may be biased, but let us look at the other side of the coin.

The degree to which people of Japanese blood have been assimilated into Hawaiian-American society has been, I feel, grossly understated. I doubt whether there is one island sociologist or anyone else familiar with the island's racial problems who will go halfway with Mr. Horlings. The statement in his opening paragraph to the effect that a majority of us cannot read or write English is plain nonsense. For the citizen group, the extent of American schooling is as high as for other racial groups in Hawaii and compares very favorably with that of the mainland states. Alien Japanese recently arrived in Hawaii do as well, on the whole, as others of like circumstances. "Thousands see or hear almost nothing American, while they consume Japanese food, Japanese clothing, Japanese music, Japanese pictures, Japanese newspapers and magazines by the shipload," says Mr. Horlings. He does not mention the overwhelming majority who prefer Bob Hope, Bette Davis, and Gary Cooper; who read the *Reader's Digest*, the *Women's Home Companion*, the *Saturday Evening Post*, *Life*, *The Nation*, *Harpers*; who dress as Americans and sing American songs. It seems silly to deny that our attitudes are fashioned after American patterns. Where Mr. Horlings gets the idea that we of Japanese blood "imagine Hawaii without American rule" and picture ourselves as top dogs in this new Hawaii, I do not know.

The question of dual citizenship cannot be dismissed so easily. As Mr. Horlings states, it is true that a great number of American citizens have failed to burn their bridges in Japan. Nonexpatriation, however, is by no means an indication of disloyalty to the United States. Many are still dependents of aliens who cannot become American citizens because of the Immigration Act of 1924 and, therefore, cannot act independently. Many have been simply negligent, for expatriation is a cumbersome and time-consuming affair. The leaders among the citizen group are all expatriated, for it is impossible to make much headway in Hawaii without taking this step. As we go into the third and fourth generations, this problem will automatically be solved.

The question of our loyalty, of course, forms the hub around which all other considerations revolve, and loyalty is too much an intangible thing to permit estimates or generalities. Most of our non-Japanese leaders have vouched for the loyalty of Hawaii's Japanese. This was borne out during and after Japan's attack on Pearl Harbor and has been officially confirmed, but Mr. Horlings prefers to judge our loyalty purely on racial lines.

What of the solution? Can we gamble on the loyalty of the 150,000 Japanese in Hawaii? I will not deny for one minute that some agents of Tokyo and their dupes are still running loose, but the overwhelming majority of us here proved that we will stand by America when the zero hour strikes. We have brothers and relatives in the armed forces of the United States and we are just as anxious for an Allied victory as other Americans.

Double or triple the FBI force in Hawaii. This would be more practical and wise than a wholesale evacuation which would involve innumerable hardships as well as seriously undermine our democratic concepts and the values of United States citizenship. That the Japanese on the West Coast have been

evacuated is no reason for the same treatment in
Hawaii. In reading through the Tolan Committee
hearings and reports, I am far from convinced such
drastic steps were necessary, especially since they
were instigated not by the military but by hysterical
civilians and interested groups. I suggest further that
we young men of fighting age be given the same
opportunities in the armed forces as other American
boys and secondly, some assurance of equality in the
post-war world.

This exchange was noted after the war in several books.
Among them Allan R. Bosworth's *American Concentration
Camps*, W. W. Norton & Co., New York, 1967, pp. 127–128;
Yankee Samurai, Joseph D. Harrington, 1979, Pettigrew En-
terprises, Inc., Detroit, Michigan, pp. 285, 333, 351; *Kodomo
No Tame Ni*, Dennis M. Ogawa, University of Hawaii Press,
1978, pp. 304–312.

In retrospect, I feel completely vindicated with the heroic
battle accomplishments of the Niseis in Europe and the
Pacific with no proven sabotage on the homefront by Japanese
Americans. I wonder, too, what Mr. Horlings himself contrib-
uted to the war effort. My purple heart speaks for me.

Detroit—War Labor Board—1943

I had completed my masters' degree in 1942 and was struggling toward my doctorate. It was a most uncomfortable
period for me as the Japanese military push in southeast Asia
was gaining spectacular success. There was no harassment of
the few Nisei students in Madison, Wisconsin but, nonetheless, we felt uneasy as reports of American casualties kept
pouring in from all fronts.

About this time, in early 1943, President Roosevelt appointed Dr. Edwin E. Witte to head the regional War Labor
Board in Detroit, Michigan. Since Dr. Witte was one of my
major professors at Wisconsin, I welcomed the opportunity to
work with him in Detroit, the "arsenal of democracy." I
decided to forego my studies until the end of the war.

I got a room at the Hannan Y.M.C.A. on East Jefferson Street near the huge Chrysler plant and went to work at the Penobscot building in downtown Detroit. As a professional economist I was able to work on many cases involving labor disputes in essential war industries. It was a wonderful opportunity to work with some of the big labor leaders and industry representatives and my oriental face was no obstacle. I gained new understanding and respect for those parties as they willingly made sacrifices in order to facilitate and expedite essential war production.

The major task of the War Labor Board at that time was to help hold down the inflationary pressures arising from the cost of labor. Labor was scarce during this period and there was an influx of workers from the south and rural areas to heavy industrial areas such as Detroit. Companies were more than willing to accommodate the demands of workers and unions, especially with the prevalence of cost-plus government contracts. The disputes that arose, therefore, were mainly between the employers and employees together on one side and the War Labor Board on the other, trying to determine what was allowable under our anti-inflationary guidelines.

I remember one particular case that exemplified the trials and tribulations of that period. It involved the Brunswick-Balk Company of Muskegan, Michigan, the leading manufacturer of billiard equipment. The company and union had agreed to a wage contract that far exceeded what was permitted by our regulations. They pleaded with me that the increases were absolutely necessary and justifiable. The highly skilled woodworkers were getting about $1.50 an hour and wanted an increase of $1.70. The morale at the plant was very low because young kids, including girls who just graduated from high school, were making more money than their skilled fathers. This was true because we allowed wages in companies producing essential war goods, such as Continental Steel in Muskegan, to rise in order to encourage workers to enter these factories. Highly skilled though the workers were at Brunswick, billiard tables could hardly be classified as essential to our war efforts, so their request was denied. To the everlasting credit of labor unions, there were very few strikes during this period, and many sacrifices were endured to maximize our war effort.

In Detroit at this time we had the first major race riot. I believe this was almost inevitable because a great migration of both white and black workers flooded Detroit and other cities in the north. As I commuted on street cars daily to work, I could feel the racial pressure building up. Orientals were not safe from this conflict, though, to my knowledge, no covert acts occurred. Still, I usually went to lunch with a fellow economist who used to be a football player at Tuskeegee Institute. He was 6'5" and 280 pounds, so we were never subjected to abuse, not even racial slurs.

On East Jefferson Street there was a "hospitality" house run by the Reverend Shigeo Tanabe, who later came to Hawaii. This house was doing a commendable job helping Niseis who came out of the relocation centers adjust to work in Detroit. It was here that I met Fumi Takata who eventually became my wife. She was working at the Harper Hospital, while her family still languished in the Amache Relocation Center in Granada, Colorado. It was the Quakers who were most active in helping the Niseis in this hostile atmosphere, as they did in all phases of the relocation fiasco. I don't think the Japanese community gave enough credit for all the good the Quakers did on behalf of the Niseis.

I left my job with the War Labor Board to join the army in early 1944. I had a general feeling of uneasiness working as a civilian, well paid and free to pursue whatever pleasure I chose. The word "civilian," as applied to a young man of draftable age, was very derogatory at that time.

Reasons for volunteering in wartime were usually couched in idealism of one sort or another. Many went in because they were drafted and had no alternative. My reasons were basically pragmatic. The first, and most compelling reason, was a visit I had from Tadao Beppu, who was in training at Camp Shelby, Mississippi. He took a leave and came all the way up to Detroit to tell me personally that Joe Takata had been killed in battle in Italy. Joe became the first Nisei fatality in Europe. Beppu, Joe Takata, Sus Tanaka, and I had lived together at 803 Wiliwili Street in the McCully area of Honolulu. We had played baseball together and had also worked for the same company. We were truly like blood brothers, and it was hard for me to continue working as a civilian from that day on.

The other major reason for leaving the War Labor Board, in what was certainly an essential job, was an unfortunate foul-up. I was informed one day that I would be put on indefinite suspension because I was being "investigated." I remained idle for about two months, and during that entire period, I received no pay. I was never once told what the grounds were or who my acusers were. I did not receive one formal letter or even an interview with an agent from the FBI or any other investigating agency. I was finally notified by my own agency to come back to work without any formal notification or apology. It was a most embarrassing experience for me and a very bitter one. My colleagues all knew I was suspended, and perhaps some had doubts about my loyalty. This experience later brought to mind my feeling of utter helplessness and disgust as I sat through some of the hearings held by Senator Joe McCarthy of Wisconsin on communist influence in the federal government. Here I witnessed innocent victims being subjected to very cruel punishment and public humiliation without the benefit of formal charges or creditable evidence. In any event, I lost all enthusiasm for my job and was glad to leave it after a few months of reinstatement.

CHAPTER 5

Off to War
1943–1946

Before the war, in the thirties, we Japanese-Americans frequently discussed among ourselves what we would do in case of a war between Japan and the United States. During the Hawaii statehood hearings, there was a cloud of suspicion that hung over the head of Niseis. This possibility was debated even more harshly outside the Japanese-American community. Albert Horlings' previously cited article is a good example. Surprisingly, Horlings' article appeared as a major piece in one of the most liberal magazines of that period, *The Nation*. Except for my own response, there were no rebuttals. The Hearst newspaper, and other jingoists, once more raised the cry of the "yellow peril." In retrospect, I now conclude that this kind of academic question can never be answered in a vacuum, although the thought of fighting for Japan was unthinkable for most of us.

Within the broad spectrum of the values we developed during our formative years in school and in our exposure to American society, specific factors inextricably guided us to make specific decisions. Peer pressure was certainly a major factor. We all registered for the draft—one by one we were being called to the colors. To have refused to participate in this ultimate test of citizenship would not have been tolerated, not only by the law but, even more importantly, by our circle of friends and relatives. In no instance did the Issei parent encourage an American son not to register for the draft or refuse induction after being called. Unlike the Vietnam War, peer and family pressure to do your part was overwhelming.

In my own case, my former housemates, Joe Takata and

Tadao Beppu, were already in uniform. When I visited Camp McCoy in Wisconsin as a student and civilian, and saw so many of my classmates preparing to go overseas with the 100th Infantry Battalion, I felt very uncomfortable. Finally, when Technical Sergeant Beppu came all the way from Camp Shelby in Mississippi to Detroit to inform me that Sergeant Joe Takata had been killed in Italy, I could no longer remain aloof.

For those Niseis with parents interned in relocation camps, I could understand their reluctance to join. Even for them, however, peer pressure was very strong. The only cases I knew of where attempts were made to evade the induction involved extreme family obligations or physical disabilities. Once in the service, a Nisei was no different from other American servicemen, only more motivated because of the special pressure of circumstances.

Military Intelligence Service Language School

World War II was commonly referred to as "total war"; unlike Vietnam, everyone and everything was involved. One only had to determine what his part would be in this united effort.

I volunteered for the army in Detroit in March 1944 even though I sincerely felt that my work as an economist for the War Labor Board was far more essential than anything I could do in the service. I was sent to Camp Savage in the outskirts of Minneapolis, Minnesota to join the Military Intelligence Service Language School. Arriving on the same train with me was Taro Suenaga, who was to remain my closest buddy at the language school. He had just completed law school at New York University. We were assigned to Company C, which was made up of Niseis from the mainland. "Kotonks," as they were called by Hawaiians, made up more than half of the student cadre.

Training at the military language school was, for the most part, a long, daily grind while I tried to memorize the Japanese characters. Following the entrance placement exams, I was placed in a very low section because my knowledge of Japa-

Camp Savage on the outskirts of Minneapolis, Minnesota

nese was poor. In addition to our texts, we went over captured documents from the South Pacific. These classroom exercises were most frustrating. The only consolation I had was to meet my new classmates from Hawaii and others from all over the mainland. Since we were in the same class almost all day long, we got to know each other very well and, even now, I cherish those memories. Occasionally we went on long marches through the Minnesota countryside, which was a welcome relief from the daily classroom grind.

While in training, I took two long furloughs. The first was to get married to Fumi, who was still working in the Social Service Department of Harper Hospital in Detroit. The wedding was presided over by the Reverend Shigeo Tanabe—he later came to Hawaii to minister in Hilo, then to Harris Memorial Church in Honolulu. Taro Suenaga was my best man and several of my buddies from Camp Savage were also in attendance. My long-time friend, Harry Oshima, came all the way from Columbia in New York to be there. The assemblage at the wedding was unique in one respect—not one relative from either side was in attendance. Mine were all in Hawaii and Fumi's relatives were all in the Amache Relocation Camp in Granada, Colorado. Our wedding dinner was at a restaurant that served sukiyaki in west Detroit. We took over the place for that night.

Following the wedding dinner, we took what may be termed a classical American honeymoon. "We shuffled off to Buffalo." The ferry left the Detroit docks about six in the evening for an overnight trip and reached Buffalo the next day in the early morning. Enroute we had a very good dance band on board and plenty of food and drink. We spent all day in the romantic surroundings of Niagra Falls and returned the next morning after another joyful evening on the ferry.

The second furlough I took was taken with my wife. I had never met her parents or her sister, Ruth. I wanted to make a trip and see firsthand what a relocation camp was like. The Amache camp was quite shocking but not unlike what I expected. The camp was indeed surrounded by barbed wire fences with guard towers at regular intervals. My wife's family was cooped up in one large room of a duplex, the rooms being divided by curtains. We ate our meals in a community mess hall much like that in the army with the same type of mess kits. However, sometimes we easily secured permission to leave camp to have our picnic lunches. Work leaves were also granted to those who wanted to go outside and earn extra money. To watch the horde of young kids as well as the elderly in the camp was to view a cross section of the Japanese community of the West Coast. The atmosphere, however, was not depressing, as the evacuees had dutifully adjusted themselves to camp life despite very trying circumstances. I doubt whether any other ethnic group could have done as well.

My father-in-law, who was in the landscaping and vegetable-buying business in Los Angeles, took up watercolor painting for the first time in his life. He discovered a talent he never knew he had. Even after he left the camp and relocated to Minneapolis, he continued to paint and took professional painting lessons. He was particularly adept at seascapes but he also had a good collection of relocation camp scenes— these were later exhibited in several art shows. A few good things like this did come out of the internment.

Following my visit with my in-laws at Amache, I continued on by myself to Sante Fe, New Mexico, to visit with my old friend and neighbor, the Japanese school teacher from Kahaluu, Mr. Giichi Sasaki. This internment camp was specifically for those who were suspected of having closer ties to Japan, such as school teachers, priests, merchants and fishermen. Mr. Sasaki was most appreciative of the bento gift I brought him from my mother-in-law. Long after the war, when I met with him again in Hawaii, he thanked me profusely for this morale-building visit.

After nine months of language study at Camp Savage, we were sent on temporary assignment to Fort McClellan in Alabama for basic training. This was my first service encounter with racial segregation. The demarcation between the white and black soldiers on busses and camp facilities within the fort was new to me. Orientals were also a segregated racial group in this army—an army which was supposed to be spreading democracy throughout the world.

After a month or so, we had a yearning for rice and oriental food. The nearest town was Anniston. I didn't think there would be a chop suey house in this little town located in the middle of nowhere, but, to my surprise, there was not one but three Chinese restaurants there serving excellent food.

On Christmas eve 1944 I was put on guard duty. It rained heavily that night and I felt foolish patrolling the camp grounds dripping wet, guarding I knew not what. However, this was the time when American soldiers were desperately fighting the "Battle of the Bulge" in France so there was an undercurrent of anxiety even at Fort McClellan.

Upon returning to Fort Snelling (the language school had moved), we began to review our lessons while we awaited our orders to ship out. Groups were usually sent out in teams of ten men, with one officer in charge, to wherever the demands for Japanese-language personnel were most needed. At about this time the American push toward Japan had reached the Philippines and the Japanese were retreating. Looking at the map of the Pacific, it appeared to me quite likely that the next big invasion would be either Taiwan or Okinawa.

I wrote a suggestion to the commandant of the language

Fort Snelling, Minneapolis, Minnesota

school that a special team be created in the event that the invasion would be in Okinawa. I noted that there were some students in his command who had lived and studied in Okinawa before the war and that were proficient not only in Japanese but also in the Okinawan dialect, which is non-intelligible to most Japanese. These students were also familiar with the geography, as well as with the customs and manners unique to the Okinawan people. I felt this special unit could be very valuable in the event of an American invasion there. My suggestion was well received by the commandant and his staff, and it was sent to G-2 headquarters in Washington and given the green light. I received a letter of commendation from the commandant.

Okinawa Campaign—1944–1945

After a check through the entire roster of students at the school, a special team of ten members was formed. I partici-

pated in the selection and those finally chosen were: S. Saki-
hara, Kazuo Nakamura, K. Miyashiro, Jiro Arakaki, K. Oshiro, H. Kobashigawa, Shinyei Gima, S. Higashi, Les Higa, and
myself—all Okinawans. Lieutenant Wallace Amioka was chosen to be our officer. We selected some men who were fluent
in the Japanese language and others who were more proficient
in the English language. The selection of Lieutenant Amioka
was very fortunate, as he was superb in all respects and he had
plenty of courage.

Departing Minneapolis, we went on by train to Fort Lewis
near Seattle, Washington, then to San Francisco for embarka-
tion. We flew to Hawaii but, to our disappointment, we were
given only one day to visit with our families. It was indeed a
joyous reunion, but we all felt the anxiety of soldiers headed
for the fighting front with all of its dangers and uncertainties.

In what may be regarded as a typical GI foul-up, our new
orders sent us to Leyte in the Philippines instead of Okinawa.
We wasted a week before flying to Okinawa following the initial American invasion on April Fools' Day 1945.

We were supposed to be a very special army team, but upon
arrival at 10th Army Headquarters off Yomitan Air Base on
Okinawa, nobody seemed to know or care about us. We were
then placed in a "pool" at headquarters to be made available
to any of the many units fighting under this command. On
temporary assignment, our boys spent most of the time
translating captured documents at headquarters. More interesting and exciting assignments included interviewing Japanese prisoners of war and civilians in protected compounds.
The POWs amused me in several ways. The Japanese military
had not established any code of behavior for men captured by
the enemy simply because they were not supposed to surrender under any circumstances. Once these soldiers gave up
their arms and were put into our prison compound, they no
longer displayed any bravado and were most cooperative.
They had little hesitancy in identifying their units, their officers and positions in the field, and they even helped us with
propaganda material we were to drop behind enemy lines.

The ability of most of our team members to speak the
Okinawan dialect proved most helpful in interrogation of Jap-

anese prisoners. This was especially valuable and effective in separating out the Japanese soldiers masquerading as Okinawan civilians. A few basic questions to them in the Okinawan dialect immediately unmasked their disguise. Very few Japanese soldiers could understand, much less speak, the dialect. They would be embarrassed when unmasked and, thereafter, would be in a more cooperative mood.

Interrogating prisoners of war was one of our main activities. This could be used to our personal advantage under certain circumstances. Since my knowledge of Japanese was very poor, I had great difficulty in translating captured documents, especially letters written in a manner which were almost impossible to decipher even with a dictionary—long hand or shorthand style. Since I had gotten to know some Japanese prisoners quite well, I decided to use their knowledge in exchange for some extra considerations. There was one particular prisoner at the Yaka compound who was a graduate of the Tokyo Imperial University, the top university in Japan. This prisoner had been hastily drafted and was disgusted to have some country bumpkin push him around. He had surrendered without resistance and gladly cooperated with me. He could, and did, easily translate in an hour or two documents that would have taken me days. I knew enough Japanese so I could determine if he was translating correctly. In this manner my translation work was not only made easier but far more accurate.

I remember one particular interview I conducted. I had the letters found on the soldier I was interviewing. As he sat before me, I read a letter sent him by his young son. It was written in simple Japanese so that even I could read it. The young boy, apparently about six or seven years old, wrote that "when I grow up I want to be a brave soldier just like my father." As the soldier hung his head in shame, I shared his pain and sorrow.

I witnessed one particularly disgusting incident in Ishikawa Village during a period when fighting was still raging in northern Okinawa. An old lady was killed and lay prone on the ground. Two American soldiers came by and with a trench knife began digging into the mouth of the old lady to collect her gold fillings. They carried a little pouch containing other items they had collected. It was a truly sickening sight and I told them so. I saw the same kind of activity involving Japanese airmen whose dead bodies were scattered after their plane crashed at the Yomitan Air Base. I'm sure Japanese soldiers also behaved in inhuman ways in countries they subjugated. I report this to indicate that soldiers of whatever nation become completely different in wartime, especially in enemy territory. It is strange how warfare affects your mental attitude. I once noticed several bodies of Japanese soldiers lying in an abandoned water reservoir in Naha. It didn't shock or bother me at all. War is truly gruesome and can turn what are otherwise decent human beings into mindless animals.

During the early phase of the Okinawan campaign, our forces captured a civilian who appeared highly educated. He was the manager of one of the big sugar refineries on Okinawa. Because of my background in economics, I was asked to interview this prisoner. This was quite a coincidence because this prisoner turned out to be Seiho Ginoza, who later changed his last name to Matsuoka. I had known him in Hawaii when he worked with my dad at the Waipahu Sugar Plantation. He went on to get a degree in engineering at the University of Chicago. He came from the same village of Kin in northern Okinawa as my family. He proved to be most useful to our military government during the occupation and was later appointed chief executive of the Ryukyu Government. After the war he became the owner of the electrical monopoly in central Okinawa and was one of the most powerful and wealthy citizens in post-war Okinawa. Seiho and I had much to talk about, but it was mostly about people he knew in Hawaii, including relatives. We also reminisced about the University of Chicago.

I had a most interesting assignment one day when a unit of the 6th Marines brought in a dozen women from their hideout in the mountains of Onna Dake. They were brought into the civilian holding station in Kin Village. Before being allowed into the compound, it was a standard requirement that everyone go through a thorough "delousing" process. Captives usually came in full of fleas and sores. In the delousing process, it was necessary, of course, to take off each piece of clothing so that the flit gun could spray the DDT to all parts of the body. As the marines tried to disrobe these women in an enclosure, they began yelling "Rape!" creating quite a commotion. It was at this point that I was called in.

After I carefully explained to them what was being done, the women were very cooperative and took off each piece of clothing at my command, and the marines immediately used the flit gun on them. "Now spread your legs," I would order and a woman would be sprayed amidst the loud laughter of the other women waiting their turn. After awhile it became a fun affair for all involved. These "comfort" girls, who were mostly from Korea and traveled with the troops, were recruited for their physical stamina and were not very attractive.

The most dangerous and valuable service our boys provided in Okinawa was to try to get the people out who were hiding in the numerous deep caves that dotted the islands. After these people were discovered, our fighting units usually called on our language men to try and talk them into surrendering peacefully by informing them that the caves would be dynamited. We succeeded on numerous occasions but failed in others. We suspected that in the caves there were Japanese soldiers mixed in with the civilians who were, as a consequence, captives who couldn't surrender even if they wanted to. I remember one case when Sergeant Kobashigawa of our team tried to evacuate a big cave in central Okinawa. He came back to camp that night in tears. He had failed to get the Japanese out and the cave was sealed. He still had many relatives living on Okinawa and he could easily imagine them buried alive with the soldiers. On the other hand, there were times when we were successful. There was no greater feeling than to watch frightened civilians meekly walk out of the caves for another lease on life. The war became very personal when civilians were involved.

During a lull I received permission to visit relatives in the northern part of the island. A lieutenant from Wisconsin, four soldiers, and I went in two jeeps to the village of Kin. I had lived in that village for six months as a child of eight and attended its elementary school. I had a vague recollection of where my relatives lived. I ventured to the house in front of what used to be my mother's house. The family that lived there, the Ikeharas, were related to my family through the marriage of my sister, Yoshiko, to one of their sons, Tatsuo. Understandably, they were frightened by our full combat uniforms. As I slowly explained who I was, they began to relax and soon were most anxious to hear about their own relatives in Hawaii. I learned, to my sorrow, that my uncle Unko was killed by the marines a few days before. This uncle of mine had lived and worked in Hawaii with my father before World War II. Ironically, he had a son in the U.S. Army whom I met in an army camp near the Golden Gate Bridge in San Francisco early in 1941. My uncle was returning from hiding in the mountains to check on the pigs and goats he had left behind. On the way home, he ran into some marines. No communication took place, as neither he nor the marines could speak the other's language. My uncle then began to run away. The marines gave chase and finally caught up with him. He hid inside the enclosure of his family tomb. The family all said that he couldn't have found a more appropriate place to die.

My aunt had also passed away the day before I arrived so I had to pay my respects. Her family's home had been completely destroyed and the family was living in the goat pen. Made of cement, it was small but clean. In the darkness inside incense was burning and the scent permeated the surrounding area. I bowed before the makeshift altar along with my other aunt and offered my condolences. She was quietly weeping in the dark and repeating: "Oh, if you could have lived only a few more days . . . your brother's son is here to visit you."

The village of Kin itself was relatively unharmed, but, nonetheless, residents were in the process of moving further north into the mountainous area. Noting their extreme hardship, I promised to bring them such essentials as salt and soap when I returned. Much to my regret, however, I was reassigned to another island soon after that and I was not able to return.

Kerama Islands—Battle of Okinawa

I was assigned next to temporary duty with an anti-aircraft unit from the New York National Guard, 866th AAA Battalion. Our headquarters was on Zamami Island, one of the three major islands in the Kerama group. Our battalion was composed of half-white and half-colored soldiers. I made it a point to mingle freely on both sides, eating my meals with each group on an alternating basis.

These islands were invaded and occupied before the main island of Okinawa. On March 26, 1945, the Third Battalion, 305th Regimental Combat Team, 77th Division, landed on Zamami and swept through the islands in five days, declaring it secured on March 31. The First Battalion of the 306th Regiment landed and occupied Tokashiki Island, the largest island in the group. The invasion was so swift and overwhelming that the Japanese forces, as well as civilians, were in total confusion and disarray. Mass suicide of civilians occurred on Zamami and Tokashiki.

The strategy of the Japanese forces was to use the Kerama Islands as the main base for their suicide boats when American forces attacked southern Okinawa. The invasion of the Keramas before Okinawa caught the Japanese by surprise. The suicide boats were completely destroyed before the huge armada of American warships arrived off the coast of Naha and Western Okinawa. Casualties among the Japanese troops were not too heavy in the Keramas since most of them fled into the mountainous, inaccessible areas.

While we were operating in the islands in June, July, and August of 1945, they were technically declared secured. Except for the towns of Zamami and Tokashiki, the Japanese forces still controlled the rest of the islands, but they remained largely inactive while hiding from, and avoiding contact with, American forces. Our main task, therefore, was to mop-up these remnants—a very nasty task as there were no discernible lines of combat and we were subject to ambush at any time.

Their reputed bravery and tenacity notwithstanding, the remaining Japanese soldiers were also realists. Faced with the

KERAMA RETTO

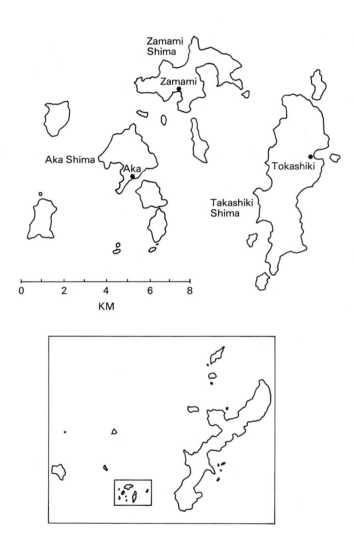

complete cut-off of supplies and ammunition, their main objective was surviving as best they could. This primarily involved raiding the native villages to replenish their steadily diminishing food supply. Their attitude toward the American mop-up forces was basically "You leave us alone and we leave you alone."

A Japanese soldier named Yasuda had surrendered on Toka-shiki Island and was brought in for interrogation in Zamami. He proved most cooperative and the information he gave me when cross checked against intelligence we already had proved him trustworthy. When I asked him whether he would accompany our patrol to the mountain range just behind the town of Tokashiki where his old unit was hiding out, he agreed without much hesitation.

A patrol of nine men was organized the next day and we set out for Tokashiki. The leader of our patrol was a black first lieutenant with eight other soldiers following. We climbed the hill back of the town before we reached No Man's Land, where land mines were laid both by the Japanese and our own troops. We intended to get closer to the enemy position so that our captive, Yasuda, could point out with greater accuracy the precise location of the Japanese troops, as well as their gun emplacements. Going through the heavily mined jungle, we had to proceed slowly and be exceedingly cautious for one misstep could set off an explosion. The lead man on the patrol was our officer. I was third and my Japanese prisoner was number four right behind me in our line of ten. I was afraid my prisoner might stray and set off a land mine so I changed places with him, telling him to follow me closely and never to get out of the line. About five minutes later, the lead man tripped a wire and a huge explosion followed. The leader was blown apart on the spot. I was knocked to the ground unconscious. When I regained my senses I felt the pain from my right chest and right leg. At that moment I was sure that it was the end for me. My prisoner escaped without a scratch. Had I kept my mouth shut for five minutes, I would have been spared. It was my turn to be unlucky.

As I was being carried down the footpath to the town of Tokashiki, a group of Okinawan farmers working their hillside fields came alongside the path for a better look at the casualties. Upon seeing me, they commented, "It is a Japanese soldier." Though in extreme pain, I had to chuckle at this ultimate irony.

Hospitals and Rehabilitation

The medics on Tokashiki Island gave me emergency care and sent me to a field hospital in southern Okinawa for major surgery. Being unable to write, I had my buddy, Ricardo Colon, write to my wife in Minneapolis. Ricardo was a black man from Schenectady, New York, who always accompanied me on patrols and acted as my bodyguard on dangerous missions. My wife later wrote me how grateful she was to get that letter before she received the telegram from the war department. In return for his favor, I promised to visit him in New York after the war. In 1950, five years later, I did go to look for him in Schenectady without having his address. My plan was to ask around in the black neighborhood for help. I spotted a black family with many children playing in their backyard. I told the lady there that I was trying to locate my wartime buddy, Ricardo Colon. Her eyes widened in amazement. He was her husband who was still in Japan with the occupation! What a coincidence! We took many pictures to send to him.

The rest of our language team was scattered on assignments with various units on the fighting front. A picture of S. Higashi appeared in newspapers in the U.S. He had found his parents while on patrol in northern Okinawa. Shinye Gima was given a messy assignment on Kume Jima where remnants of Japanese naval forces were executing native leaders who had cooperated with American troops. He himself was threatened but escaped unharmed to eventually return home to become a professor at the University of Hawaii. Jiro Arakaki found his parents in one of the civilian compounds. All members of our team eventually met up with relatives. These were some of the happy endings for all of us at the tragic end of the war in the Pacific.

Lieutenant Amioka became a kind of hero for he captured

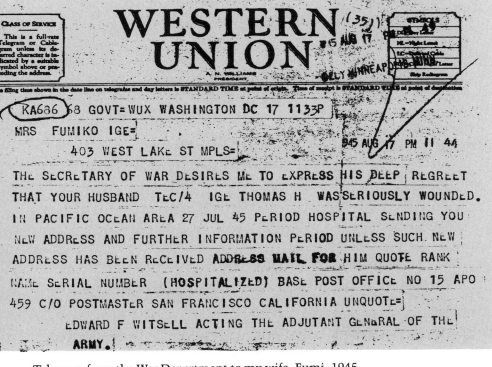

Telegram from the War Department to my wife, Fumi, 1945

and killed the leader of the Japanese soldiers hiding out and raiding the villages of northern Okinawa. This Japanese air force colonel was the most feared and hated tyrant, even for the native civilians struggling to survive in the mountains.

From the field hospital in Okinawa I was put on board a navy hospital ship bound for Ulithi in the South Pacific. This was quite an experience. The war casualties on board were a tragic lot with the serious cases bedded near the fan tail so they could be easily disposed of when they passed away. I was with this group. Despite all the agony and pain, men were relieved and happy at the thought of going home at last. There was one marine with a bullet lodged in his head, walking around gingerly and looking forward to resuming his studies at Johns Hopkins University in Baltimore. Others displayed

Mrs. Fumiko Ige   U.S.S. OCONTO APA 187
403 West Lake Street,   c/o Fleet Post Office
Minneapolis (8), Minnesota.   San Francisco, Calif.

Dear Mrs. Ige:

    I wish to inform you that your husband who was wounded on 27 July 1945
is making fair progress. He has shrapnel wounds of the chest, right arm and
right leg, and his present condition is serious. Please be assured that he is
receiving the best possible medical care on this ship.

                              Sincerely yours,

                              P. JACKSON
                              Captain, U.S.N.R.
                              Commanding Officer.

Letter from Captain P. Jackson aboard ship bound for Ulithe

such courage that made it easier for me to withstand my own
pain.

From Ulithi we were transferred to another ship for a short
trip to the navy hospital in Guam. While being transferred, I
clearly remembered how proud I was as the loudspeaker
announced "War casualties passing through" and all the servicemen stood at attention and saluted us.

At the hospital in Guam a follow-up surgery was performed
on me, and, after that, it was just a matter of waiting for the
wounds to heal. I was being given a steady dose of morphine
to ease the pain and I began to feel strong again. The only
noteworthy event that occurred while awaiting shipment
stateside occurred on the day following Japan's surrender on
August 15, 1945. Just off to the north of Guam is the small
island of Rota, called "Rat Island" by the Americans, where
Japanese soldiers were still holding out. Since these soldiers
were in no position to do us any harm, they were left alone.
Our battleships used that island for target practice and when
our bombers returned from missions to Japan, they always
unloaded their unused bombs on this island. It was the assess-
ment of our command on Guam that there couldn't be many

Japanese soldiers left there since their food supply had been cut off for some time. With the surrender, two troop ships were sent to evacuate survivors. To our utter surprise, over a thousand soldiers surrendered. They were assembled in front of our hospital, and I watched as the emperor's surrender message was read to them. It was a most solemn ceremony, and many of the soldiers were crying. The war was finally over for all of us, and there was a steady display of fireworks on Guam.

The sudden end of the war, however, caused an immediate change in the use of our transportation facilities, and stateside return of war casualties was put at the bottom of the priority list. After a few months of frustration, I was finally flown to Hickam Air Force Base Hospital for a brief stay. My family and friends were able to visit me and it was a happy reunion despite my inability to get up and move around. They were relieved that I could still smile and keep up my morale. As much as I wanted to get out to see Hawaii after being away for five years, this was not permissible under the circumstances.

The next stop was at the Shick Army Hospital in Clinton, Iowa, between Dubuque and Davenport, on the Mississippi River. This was good for me because my wife and her family were living in Minneapolis—a two-hour train ride to Clinton on the Rock Island Railroad. I do not recall the details of our emotional reunion but I know there was no party of any kind. While still fighting in Okinawa, I wrote Fumi that we were going to have a once-in-a-lifetime celebration on my return, but her tears of joy were more than enough for me. Recuperating in a hospital was a necessary waste of time. Once I began walking around, I enjoyed new friendships with veterans from various war fronts.

When I was finally able to maneuver on my crutches, I made a side trip to Madison, Wisconsin to renew my acquaintance with the economics staff at the University and to make plans to resume my studies. I had already been promised a scholarship as a teaching assistant in the department. I was given a warm reception; they were all familiar with the trials and tribulations before and during the war of the "boy from Hawaii."

From Clinton, Iowa, the next and last hospital stop was to

NATIONAL WAR LABOR BOARD
DEPARTMENT OF LABOR BUILDING
WASHINGTON, D. C.

Sgt. Thomas H. Ige
Schick General Hospital
Clinton, Iowa   December 10, 1945

Dear Ige:

From a letter of Miss Bridgman received from Madison, I learned
that you were wounded at Okinawa and are now undergoing hospital treatment. I am writing this letter to express the hope that you will soon
be entirely well again. From Miss Bridgman's letter, it appears that
you were in Madison but need further hospital treatment. I also get
from her letter that it is your intent to return to Wisconsin to complete
your graduate work after you are discharged from the service.

I have always admired your action of going into the military service. I know that this was your own choice and that you knew you were
going into a type of service involving a great deal of risk. You did
suffer injury but I hope that this will not have serious lasting effects;
also, that you soon will be fully recovered.

Sincerely,

Edwin E. Witte

Letter from Edwin E. Witte while I was recovering from war wounds in
Schick General Hospital, Clinton, Iowa

be the big Percy Jones Hospital in Battle Creek, Michigan.
This time the emphasis of my stay was on rehabilitation in
preparation for return to civilian life. As most of the patients
were relatively healthy, recreational and vocational activities
were readily available and encouraged. We went to the gym to
shoot basketball and U.S.O. shows were held frequently at
night. If we were interested there was a long list of vocations
we could participate in: carpentry, repairing electrical equipment, clerical help, mechanics, plumbing, and so on.

Since my post-discharge course was well defined, I chose to
take piano lessons. This turned out to be far more fun than I
had anticipated. Spending three to four hours every day, one
can progress quite rapidly and I was beginning to really enjoy
my practice sessions when the medical board decided I was
ready for discharge. As a temporary soldier you anxiously
await the day when they grant you an honorable discharge. I
would have been more than happy to cradle that certificate

with my termination pay and rush up to Minneapolis to be with my wife. Surprisingly, the medical board gave me a forty-percent disability rating as well. Throughout the rest of my life I stood to collect about a quarter of a million dollars—far more than I ever collected while in service!

Upon my discharge I joined my wife and her family in Minneapolis, Minnesota. My father-in-law had left the Amache Relocation Camp in Colorado and had taken a job as a head gardener for the Metropolitan Life Insurance Company's headquarters. My wife, Fumi, worked at the University of Minnesota in the security office headed by "Chick" Hanscomb who was to become a very close family friend. Fumi was well suited for this position. She had worked for the Los Angeles Police Department before the war. The University of Minnesota, with all its related activities including the hospital and farms, was like a city within a city necessitating a large security force. In his privileged position, Mr. Hanscomb was able to get us choice seats for all university activities. This included tickets on the fifty-yard line for all home football games. As they had a good football team in 1946, with stars like Leo Nomelini, Clayton Tonnemaker, Bud Grant, Gordy Sotour, and Billy Bye, we thoroughly enjoyed these games.

Since this brief sojourn was in the summer of 1946 and my assignment at the University of Wisconsin did not begin until that fall, I spent the time studying German at the University of Minnesota. I abhorred language studies, but proficiency in German was required, and I had to hurdle this requirement in order to obtain a Ph.D. I grunted and groaned the entire summer, but it paid off later, much to my relief. That summer Minneapolis was a most pleasant experience in comparison to the army days at Camp Savage and Fort Snelling.

Concluding Remarks on the Okinawan Campaign

For those of us of Okinawan descent, fighting with the American forces in Okinawa was a very trying experience. In addition to the physical aspect of the war, the spiritual toll war took was even harder to bear. In the eyes of frightened civilians hiding in caves or escaping on coral roads, we could sense the tragedies of these people and well imagine what the fate of our own families would have been like if they had not emigrated to Hawaii. During the course of the campaign, all of us on the team visited with relatives and shared their sufferings and anxiety firsthand. Looking back, one might be grateful that they emerged as well as they did; but in the very midst of the battle, everything looked so dark and foreboding. Reflecting back on this bitter campaign, I have several thoughts.

I don't think the role played by our commanding general, Simon Boliva Buckner, has been properly appreciated. He was criticized for his delaying tactics when America was in a hurry to end the war. On several occasions he halted the American advance in the southern sector of Okinawa so that civilians entrapped could safely escape to the north. This saved thousands of lives from needless death. On June 11, 1946, General Buckner sent a letter to Lieutenant General Mitsuru Ushijima, Commanding General of the 32nd Army of the Japanese defense forces, urging negotiations for surrender. I still recall reading that letter, which was widely circulated on both sides. It was the tone of the letter that greatly impressed me. There was no trace of arrogance or a condescending tone.

General Buckner laid out in full detail the hopelessness of the Japanese forces' situation: no resupply of arms or other materials necessary to carry on the war, the complete destruction of their naval and air support. He reminded the Japanese general of the military tradition and history of great generals of the past who surrendered under hopeless odds in order to spare the needless death of their compatriots. Japanese forces were no longer fighting in organized patterns. They were scattered and were only trying to survive. The Japanese general refused to negotiate. In the meantime, the more realistic Japanese commanders under him took their own lives. They were Rear Admiral Minoru Ota of the Okinawan Naval Base Forces, Lieutenant General Takeo Fujioka, Commanding General of the 62nd Division, and Lieutenant General Tokutaro Nakajima of the 63rd Division. All of them killed themselves before General Ushijima and his deputy Lieutenant General, Isamu Oho, surrendered and killed themselves on June 23rd at the mouth of their cave headquarters on Mabuni Dake. General Ushijima's decision cost an average of 2,000 Japanese soldiers' lives every day, along with thousands of civilians, including the now-famous Himeyuri nurses. As I visited the memorial to these martyred nurses recently, I was unable to forgive General Ushijima for their deaths.

I would also like to point out that the dilemma and predicament of the village leaders in Okinawa was very tragic. As the American forces captured and secured towns and villages, a dangerous situation was created. During the day the American forces could be seen and respected, but when they withdrew for the night, Japanese soldiers hiding in the mountains would descend to the villages looking not only for food but, more dangerously, for those who had cooperated with the captors. Of necessity, village leaders worked with Americans to get food and medical supplies. In the mountainous area of Yanbaru, these village leaders were singled out for execution by the night raiders from the mountains. One can laugh at the antics of village leaders as portrayed in the "Tea House of the August Moon," but as it happened, especially in remote areas, the leaders were placed in a tragic dilemma. This dilemma in the villages was also inevitable in captured and occupied areas in Europe and in Vietnam. To experience this firsthand was most disturbing.

All through the Okinawan campaign, especially toward the end, there was considerable preparation for the invasion of Japan itself. Japanese prisoners were interrogated on such things as the shorelines of Kyushu and other potential landing sites in Japan. I was, and am today, very skeptical that such an invasion would have taken place and whether this would have been necessary with the inevitable loss of millions of lives. Thousands of heavy bombers were flying almost unmolested to rain wholesale destruction throughout the major industrial centers of Japan. Even by Japanese accounts, remaining military resources were limited and deteriorating rapidly. Postwar reports indicated that Japanese leaders were indeed cognizant of inevitable defeat and were attempting to end the war using Russia as the intermediary. In light of these revelations, I remain very skeptical of our justification for dropping atomic bombs on Hiroshima and Nagasaki. Even without this holocaust, I am convinced that Japan would have surrendered within a year if we had continued our relentless bombing and total destruction of its civilized society. The battle of Okinawa was the Waterloo for Japan.

The value of the contribution made by the Nisei language men was certainly very evident, but to claim, as some do, that we shortened the war by two years and saved millions of lives is a needless exaggeration. Compared to the heroic deeds of our brethren on the European front, ours really must be considered rather minor.

CHAPTER 6

Back to Civilian Life 1946

University of Wisconsin

The return to Wisconsin after the war was a happy contrast to the fall of 1941, when I first arrived there with no money, no connections, and fuzzy ideas about what I was doing. This time I had good living quarters, for veterans had housing in an exclusive trailer camp at Camp Randall, located in the sports complex of the University, next to the football stadium and the basketball field house. The economics department of the University was Sterling Hall, only a five minute walk from the trailer camp. I had the GI bill and allowances, the GI disability pay, and a small salary as teaching assistant to boot.

My graduate work within the department was also far more pleasant than in the past. By this time I had gotten to know the professors on a personal basis and I had completed most of the basic courses. The University of Wisconsin had a reputation for being a very friendly and informal place among the big schools. I found this to be true, at least on the graduate level. I cite one small incident as an example. It was in 1942 when rationing was in full force and some things were hard to get. One day I was in the men's bathroom. To my surprise my economic theory professor, Dr. James Early, was standing right next to me. He asked me how I was getting along. I told him everything was fine except I was having difficulty buying toothpaste. During rationing, in order to get a new tube of toothpaste, you had to hand in an old, used one. Somehow in my carelessness I had discarded my old tube and I was in a quandary. The next day, after class, Dr. Early called me aside and to my surprise gave me an old, used toothpaste tube. I was most surprised and grateful. About twenty years later, while I was running a summer program in economics at the University of Hawaii for high school teachers, I invited Dr. Early as visiting expert for the four-weeks session. In the opening class, I introduced Dr. Early to the school teachers and told them of the incident and why he was such a good friend. He was, of course, somewhat taken aback, as he had completely forgotten about the incident.

Most of my upper-level graduate courses were in what was referred to as seminars. These classes rarely had more than twenty students in them. We sat around tables to facilitate class discussions. All of us were required to make two or three reports during the semester, followed by open discussions. The professor in charge ran the class more like the chairman at a meeting, though he would discourse on some pertinent topic about half of the time. One couldn't hide in these classes and, before long, the better students usually stood out. We got to know each other very well too.

In addition to my classes in the economics department, I chose to minor in law. The classes I took in the law school overlapped with economics. They included labor law and industrial relations, fair trade and monopoly, public utility, and taxation. The professors in the law school worked with the professors in the economics department on public issues and legislation. This was a very active faculty working in harmony with the Progressive Party of the LaFollet brothers. It was said of the University campus that its borders were the entire state. This was later to reach beyond the state to the entire nation with the TVA projects of Dr. Glaeser. Dr. Witte was appointed by President Roosevelt to head the staff of the congressional committee that drew up the Social Security Act in the mid-thirties and later to head the Regional War Labor Board in Detroit during World War II. Dr. Harold Groves was in Washington consulting on tax matters. It was no accident that one of his proteges was Dr. Walter Heller, the leading economist in Washington during the Truman, Kennedy, and Johnson administrations. Dr. Nate Feinsinger of the law school was very active in labor disputes of national emergency status, which included the major waterfront strikes on the Pacific Coast. Dr. Feinsinger was later appointed by President Kennedy to head the National Wage Stabilization Board in Washington. I joined him there in 1952–1953. Working with professors of this caliber, economics became a very dynamic subject and the tendency was to become partisan rather than remain purely objective or simply an observer on the sidelines. Many universities and professors frowned on being partisan as being "unprofessional."

I came to know and like Dr. Feinsinger well, and in later years, while at the University of Hawaii, I invited him to come over for some of the programs I conducted there for the University and the U.S. State Department. It was a great joy for me to be able to repay these professors for at various times most of them visited Hawaii, usually as visiting professors. Without exception, they enjoyed their brief sojourn in Hawaii.

While doing my graduate internship, my son was born in 1947 in Madison. I named him Martin after the professor who gave me a research assistantship in 1942 when I was really struggling. I recall one rather amusing incident as my wife awaited the birth of our son. While my wife shared a waiting room at the Wisconsin General Hospital, she began discussing with her roommate names for their babies. Fumi remarked that she abhorred naming a child after its father with a "Junior." Much to my wife's embarrassment, we learned a little later that this lady named her baby "Oscar Meyer the Third!"

Completing my Ph.D.

The last hurdles I had to clear before leaving the Wisconsin campus were the preliminary examination, which took three full days, then the French and German language exams. These language requirements were really a nuisance and, I believe, were required only to make it more difficult to get a Ph.D. Languages were a standard requirement in practically all major universities, however. There was a widely circulated

University of Wisconsin, 1950. *Brothers and parents, left to right:* Hiroshi, Dad, Kosuburo, Tom, cousin Helen, Mother

story at that time about a graduate student at Wisconsin who had spent some time in a university in Berlin. During the course of his exam in German, he and his examiner got into a heated argument about the Nazi regime. They argued hot and long in the German language, but in the process he failed to pass the language barrier, and he had to take the test over with another professor. With these and other obstacles out of the way, I was ready to start my long journey as a professor. The remaining requirement of the thesis was met while teaching full time away from the Wisconsin campus.

On to Minnesota—1947

Obtaining that first job is always an exciting experience for all graduate students. We were very fortunate in the late forties— veterans were returning in great numbers to the universities throughout the country and the demand for college professors mushroomed. It was a seller's market. I chose to go to the

University of Minnesota, Duluth Branch, Department of Business and Economics, 1950. *Left to right, back row:* Mitchell Locks, A.M.; Cecil H. Meyers, Ph.D.; John A. Dettmann, M.S. *Front row:* Bruce C. Netschert, Ph.D.; Thomas H. Ige, Ph.D.; Richard O. Sielaff, Ph.D. (dept. head); Arthur M. Clure, Li.B.

Duluth Branch of the University of Minnesota. This was similar to the Hilo branch of the University of Hawaii. The former Duluth State Teachers College had been converted to a four-year college under the same board of regents as the main university.

For a boy from Hawaii, life in Duluth was a big change and challenge. This "ice box" would be 40 degrees below zero on many days during the winter, and during my first year, we had six consecutive weeks of sub-zero weather. I often wondered why I was enduring these hardships when I could be in sunny Hawaii. When you are young and adventuresome, however, you can take these drastic changes as part of life's journey.

Except for the weather, I was fortunate in several respects. Of the two thousand students, mostly from the Iron Range and the Twin Ports area, many were returning veterans who had gone through the same war experience as I had. This fact

alone brought down whatever racial barriers there might have
been between me and this predominantly Scandinavian population. There really was more feeling of camaraderie among
veterans than I had expected. Students took me fishing and
we frequently golfed together.

I have always had a fascination for politics. My years at
Duluth were no exception. This was strong Democratic country—in the old days it was the International Workers of the
World (IWW); then the party was later changed to the Farmer-
Labor Party which was part of the national Democratic organization. In the year I settled there, a big battle was being
waged by Hubert H. Humphrey for the U.S. Senate. He had
been a big success as mayor of Minneapolis. My wife and I
actively participated in his northern Minnesota organization
and got to make many new and valuable contacts not otherwise possible. The students at the Duluth branch of the University were also very active politically and we worked on
many projects together. We later basked in the glory of the
overwhelming triumphs of Humphrey and the Farmer-Labor
Party.

Fumi and I were especially fortunate in finding a good place
to live in the midst of the post-war housing shortage. The
U.S. Department of Interior decided to abandon the fish
hatchery on the Lester River in the outskirts of Duluth. The
facilities were ceded to the state and the University of Minnesota became the beneficiary. The hatchery no longer operated.
The house formerly occupied by the director became available
to the University and I became the lucky inheritor of it. The
house was located on London Road, a very fashionable part of
the city bordering Lake Superior. This road continued on to
Canada as the North Shore Drive, one of the most scenic
drives in the United States.

This house was to provide some of my most memorable
experiences while living in Duluth. Our most exciting experiences were the run-ins with the big black bears. One particularly dry summer, when the bears were badly wanting for
food, they descended into the city. Our house, being on the
outer edge of the city, was a favorite foraging place. Big bears
weighing up to six hundred pounds came quite regularly at

night to turn over the garbage cans. They were quite friendly, and the conventional wisdom regarding them was, "You don't hurt them, they don't hurt you." Watching them roam freely in your backyard, however, gave you an uneasy feeling. In a downtown Duluth hotel on Superior Street, there was a great big stuffed bear in the lobby. The story goes that it had wandered into the hotel one summer. It is hard to believe, but it could be true. *Life* magazine had a series of pictures showing the wanderings of the black bears in Duluth. In a series of photographs, the first panel showed three big black bears swimming in Duluth harbor, somewhat lost. The next panel pictured three firemen going to their rescue in a boat. The third panel showed the bears approaching the boat. The last panel showed the three bears in the boat and the three firemen desperately swimming to shore.

My favorite bear story took place at Lester Park golf course, located about a mile from where I lived and also a favorite place for the black bears to roam. At that time I was just a beginner in golf and had a hard time breaking a hundred. I used to tell my friends I was breaking eighty quite regularly to their disbelief. This was true because on many holes the black bears would be gathered around the tee. Although the saying was if you don't harm them, there is nothing to fear, with a big bear nearby watching you make a big swing with your driver, he might think you were making an unfriendly act. The wiser thing to do, I thought, would be to skip that hole. Even on the fairways a bear frequently and unexpectedly would come out of the woods to inspect your ball. Here again, it was better not to argue with the bear but to go to the next hole. I was lucky to play twelve holes, and breaking eighty was not hard to score.

The timber wolves also came wandering onto the frozen ice in front of our house. The Lester River itself was a source of adventure when the smelt began to run. We used to catch buckets full. My in-laws would come up from Minneapolis to get in on the smelt run and we would fry the smelt in deep fat for a most delicious dinner.

While teaching at the University, I also had the onerous task of finishing my dissertation. I did this mainly during

summer vacations. I would leave my family, get a room at the
YMCA in Madison, and work day and night. For two summers
I did this, sacrificing time with my family. I finally finished in
1949, to the relief of all. My professors, especially Dr. Witte,
my sponsor, were most helpful and encouraging. In this
respect, too, I feel I was very lucky. About twenty-five percent
of all Ph.D. candidates never complete their dissertations and
remain frustrated for the rest of their lives.

The title of my dissertation was "Pension Plans Under Collective Bargaining." Most Ph.D. dissertations lie buried in
libraries with scant attention ever paid to them. In the post-
war period, beginning with John L. Lewis and the United
Mine Workers, pensions and welfare benefits became major
issues in bargaining. In the private sector, the mine workers
and a few unions in the construction industry, like the International Brotherhood of Electrical Workers (IBEW), had successfully negotiated a pension plan. There were many technical, as well as legal, problems in this relatively new area of
collective bargaining. The United Auto Workers, as well as
the Steel Workers Union, were pushing hard for pension programs in their contracts. I was paid by the Steel Workers
Union to consult with them on pension programs they were
in the process of negotiating. I do not claim to have had any
substantial effect on what eventually evolved, but having
gone to the Pittsburgh headquarters of the powerful Steel
Workers Union as a paid consultant has always been a source
of pride for me.

One other major incident of some significance occurred
during my stay at Duluth. It involved a labor dispute. The
Duluth Steam Corporation, which provided heat for downtown buildings and St. Luke's and St. Mary's hospitals, was in
a deadlock in its contract negotiations. Its twenty-one workers belonged to the International Union of Operating Engi-
neers, Local 516, AFL. The issues involved wage increases,
insurance, health, and welfare benefits.

I received a request from Governor Luther Youngdahl of
Minnesota to chair a fact-finding commission to try and settle
the strike. I don't know how he got my name, but, in view of
the threat of a strike that would virtually cripple the city and
cause irreparable damage, I accepted this assignment. Repre-

senting labor on this commission was William F. Wright of St. Paul with Bradley Mahana representing industry. After two days of hearings and arguments, we made the recommendations that became the basis for the final settlement reached a few days later. The governor sent me a warm letter of appreciation, and the provost of the University said I rendered a very valuable service. Trying to arbitrate, or mediate, a labor dispute is a very thankless job and, after that, I tried to avoid it whenever possible. I settled a few other relatively minor disputes on the Iron Range and was kept on the governor's panel of arbitrators while in Minnesota.

During this time we had our second child, Dianne. Orientals were very scarce in northern Minnesota, so doctors in the area had virtually no experience delivering oriental babies. My daughter was born with a noticeable birth mark on her lower back. This was a blue mark, generally referred to as the "Mongolian Strain." This was, and is, very common in oriental babies and always disappears as the child grows older. Being a rare phenomenon, doctors from all over northern Minnesota came into observe this strange mark. I like to tease Dianne now that more people examined her *okole* (posterior) than for any other baby.

The Wage Stabilization Board

The Korean War broke out in the summer of 1950 and once again I was called to work with the Wage Stabilization Board in its regional office in Minnesota. Since the work was similar to what I had done at the War Labor Board in Detroit during the early part of World War II, I felt obligated to accept this new assignment. My in-laws still lived in Minneapolis so we moved in with them for the duration. The job became rather monotonous as the war began to stabilize, however. When my old law professor, Dr. Feinsinger of Wisconsin, asked me to join his staff, I readily accepted and moved the family to Alexandria, Virginia. This was my first stay near our nation's capital, and we were quite excited about all the opportunities available there.

In connection with my work, my most memorable recol-

DR. THOMAS H. IGE
Brotherhood Speaker

A Brotherhood week meeting will be held at 7:30 p. m. Tuesday in Steelworkers' hall by the Duluth Industrial council. Dr. Thomas H. Ige, assistant professor of economics, University of Minnesota, Duluth branch, will speak on "Labor's Place in Tomorrow's Democracy."

Commission Files Report

Pay Hike Recommended For Steam Corp. Workers

A pay increase of 7½ cents an hour, retroactive to last Nov. 15, was recommended today for employes of the Duluth Steam Corp., by a fact-finding commission appointed by Governor Youngdahl.

The commission also urged that representatives of the company and their unions meet to work out an agreement on insurance, health and welfare program to cost a minimum of 5 cents an hour, the Associated Press reported in St. Paul.

jobs in the most comparable firm in the area.

"It takes into consideration the profit picture of the company as well as the general wage increase grants in the area."

Members of the commission were Thomas H. Ige, Duluth, for the public; Bradley Mahana, St. Paul, for industry, and William F. Wright, St. Paul, for labor.

lection was observing the antics of the great John L. Lewis of the United Mine Workers. I had read so many colorful stories about this labor baron that it was a big treat for me to see him operate at very close range. The union and mine operators had agreed to a contract that had yet to be approved by the Wage Board. The wage settlement was far beyond what was allowable under our general guidelines. Even before he stepped into the building, the news was out that John L. was to make a personal appearance before the Board. We all awaited him anxiously as if he were a great movie celebrity.

True to form, he belittled and ridiculed the Board in his inimitable way, stating that whatever the Board decided, he would get the full wage increase for his workers. Furthermore, he promised that while he vacationed in the Caribbean, the Board would disintegrate. He was a massive individual and his trademark was his bushy eyebrows. When he thundered, he was like a king making royal pronouncements. He dressed like a tycoon, too. He wore white gloves and was driven around by a black chauffeur in a big Cadillac. As he prophesied, he got all he wanted and the Board and all its regulations were soon abandoned. This was, however, due more to the fact that the Korean War was ending, and there was a general clamor in Washington to phase out all economic controls related to the war economy.

In Washington, I also had the opportunity to see Senator Joseph McCarthy conduct his infamous inquiries into Communist penetrations within the federal government. The hearing room itself felt ominous. You had the feeling that you were about to witness a lynching. As the Senator and his counsel, Roy Cohn, took turns badgering the witnesses, you felt utterly helpless—the bullying seemed to continue endlessly. The Senator had a flair for dramatics and he took every opportunity to slander and ruin the reputations of his victims, whom he chose almost at random. I got a better appreciation of due process by watching this committee operate outside the confines of acceptable courtroom procedure, feeling free to make a mockery of justice. McCarthy really set the stage for the widespread witch-hunting of that period.

I remember one witness in particular who had worked in

various federal agencies for a number of years. I think his
name was Harris. The Senator's accusations were based primarily on a book Harris had written while he was a student at
Columbia University in New York. He had written the book
entitled "King Football" in the mid-thirties when pro-Soviet
sentiment was fashionable among the radical elements in
New York. During the grilling, Harris kept asking Senator
McCarthy to relate his questions to some area of his work or
activities during all the years since he had left Columbia University but to no avail. In a similar fashion, my former professor of economics at the University of Hawaii, Dr. William
Taylor, was singled out and practically ruined because he
worked for the U.S. Treasury Department in China and had
had some dealings with the Communists there in the thirties.
Having known Dr. Taylor, I would vouch for his integrity and
loyalty.

CHAPTER 7

Back to Hawaii

University of Hawaii 1953–1980

After being away for thirteen years, I finally returned to Hawaii in the fall of 1953. It was a dream come true for me—in fact, better than a dream, for though I knew I would return someday, I never thought it would be as a professor at the University of Hawaii, my alma mater. I was to remain at the University for twenty-six years until my retirement at the age of 63 in 1980.

Because there is misunderstanding about the work and life of a university professor, let me pause here to clarify a few points. The outstanding feature of a professor's job at almost any large university is the degree of freedom and flexibility he or she is able to enjoy. This freedom and flexibility is what makes professorship at a university so attractive, even if less financially rewarding than other professions. I will relate here the various assignments I experienced while performing my primary duty of lecturing at the University—extensive trips throughout Asia, assignments to Tokyo and Washington, D.C., summer exchanges to Wisconsin and Cincinnati, and a research trip to Bolivia.

Flexibility begins with your assignment within the university department. The courses you conduct are tailored to your area of concentration and do not vary much during the year or from year to year. My courses were Micro and Macro Economics (undergraduate and graduate), Money and Banking, and, occasionally, Quantitative Methods, and Social Legislation. The lecture hours were very flexible, suited to accommodate both the professor and the university. It may surprise some people to learn that a professor may lecture only on Mondays,

Wednesdays, and Fridays or on Tuesdays, Thursdays, and Saturdays. This is the general pattern. Students also arrange their courses so that they may be on the campus for only three days a week. This arrangement helps to ease traffic problems, as well as the lack of classroom space. For most professors this accounts for nine to twelve hours of lecturing a week, and for the students, twelve to sixteen credit hours. For both professors and students this certainly is not the full extent of their work load. The students generally study two to three hours for each credit hour of lecture. It is no less for the professor. For both student and professor, it does not matter where, when, or how one prepares for classes.

For me, I found nights and weekends most productive because there were fewer interruptions which allowed for better concentration. When friends saw me golfing on some weekdays, they wondered why I wasn't at work. I could better prepare my lectures or do research at home at night. This is true for many students as well. When telephone calls went unanswered at my office, very often it was because I was lecturing in the classroom. Office hours, of course, were different. Even on my off-lecture days, opportunities were provided for student consultations within regularly posted office hours.

How a professor spends the summer months, June, July, and August, is generally left to his or her discretion. Rarely does one take a vacation for the entire period as some may suspect. In our department, as in most departments, you were permitted to teach one summer session out of two with additional compensation which was less than the rate of pay during the regular academic year. I cannot recall a single year when I took a vacation for the entire summer. An attractive alternative was to go to some other university to lecture for the summer. On exchanges I went to the University of Wisconsin, Xavier University in Cincinnati, and Waseda University in Tokyo. I feel these experiences did me and the University a great deal of good.

We also had the sabbatical leave privilege, which accrued after every six years. During a sabbatical leave you received six months at full pay or a full year at half pay. I went on sabbatical to do research work in Bolivia. Leave of absence without pay was also allowed, provided the purpose of the leave benefited the university. On this basis I went to work for U.S. Senator Daniel K. Inouye in Washington, D.C., as well as took extensive trips throughout Asia for the Asian Studies Program and for the East-West Center. On temporary assignments within the University, I served as director of the Economic Research Center as well as director of the Asian Studies Program and head of the Economic Education Program. I even substituted as temporary replacement for Dr. Shunzo Sakamaki's summer program and Henry Vasconcello's athletic directorship. One can see that my twenty-six years at the University was not one continuous stretch of teaching in one department.

Asian Studies—East-West Center—1958–1960

My first big assignment away from my regular position in the Department of Economics occurred in 1958 when I was appointed as the first director of a newly created Asian Studies Program. This experience turned out to be almost bizarre from the start. The Asian Studies and Overseas Operations Programs were moved through our legislature by a strong coalition of scholars interested in various aspects of Asian studies, even though these programs were not included in the requests by the Board of Regents. The Board itself was not opposed to these new programs—the programs were simply very low on their priority list. Professor Charles Moore, head of the Philosophy Department and the prime force behind the long established and very successful East-West Philosophers' conferences, met me casually on campus one day and told me confidentially that the president of the University, Dr. Lawrence Snyder, was going to call me in and make me a proposition. I had absolutely no idea what he was talking about. Professor Moore advised me not to turn down the president's request. When I was finally called in, President Snyder said that he would like to appoint me as head of the Asian Studies Program. This was a complete surprise and shock to me, and I said, in essence, "Why me?" I have never had much experi-

Asian Studies For Asians

By Dr. Thomas H. Ige

Professor of Economics, University of Hawaii
Director, U.H. Asian Studies Program

INVITING a Vietnamese and an Indonesian or some other native Asian to come to Hawaii for Asian studies sounds like an absurd idea. Why should an Asian come to Hawaii or the United States to study about Asia? Don't the Asians know more about their own area than Americans do?

Even if we grant the desirability of such a program, why in **Hawaii** instead of Chicago or some place in Asia itself?

The basic idea of Asian studies for Asians and some of the best answers to the above questions are actually coming from the Asian educators themselves.

This was one of the surprising impressions I got on my recent trip t h r o u g h Southeast Asia.

RASH OF PROGRAMS

The rash of Asian Studies programs among American universities in the post-World War II period has been aimed primarily at Americans for a better understanding of Asia. This, of course, is very logical and necessary.

Some of the big blunders mentioned in "The Ugly American" could have been

Dr. Ige recently made a trip to Southeast Asia to further the University of Hawaii's Asian Studies program.

spared if we had put more emphasis on Asian Studies for Americans.

Our own Asian Studies program at the University is l i k e w i s e geared to the needs of our own students for a better understanding of Asia, and perhaps for more effective overseas operations. If we can add to this a major emphasis on Asian Studies for Asians, we would have a program unique among American universities and of great significance for the proposed East-West center.

LOGIC AND APPEAL

The logic and appeal behind Asian Studies for Asians is this:

1—Most of the countries in Asia emerged from colonialism in the very recent past. They had been isolated, with a minimum of communication and cultural exchange among themselves.

As a result, I was told in Saigon, for example, that Vietnamese know much about France and Europe, a little about America, but very little about neighbor Thailand to the west or Malaya to the immediate south, or about Asia in general.

The need to know more about their next-door neighbors was expressed to me in Malaya, Indonesia, Thailand, and even in Japan. Asian educators are certainly frank in their assertion that Americans know more about Asia as a whole than do Asians themselves. the use of educational institutions and programs for purposes of propaganda. They are sophisticated and can spot a phony program.

Our own courses dealing with the philosophies, religions, anthropology, history, and languages of Asia will, I believe, clearly reveal two things:

First, there is a greater common heritage among these new nations than is commonly realized. Greater appreciation of this point alone will soften some of the sharp edges of the new spirit of nationalism (e.g., Cambodia v. Thailand; Indonesia v. the Philippines; Malayans v. Chinese, etc.).

Second, this common heritage is completely foreign and antagonistic to the ideologies of communism. The latter point need not be propagandized; it should become self-evident.

The fact that Americans of Asian descent have been able to get along so well among themselves in Hawaii impresses the Asians very strongly.

We have learned at the University that the first big adjustment problem of the Asian Fulbright scholars who come to us for orientation is with other Asians. As this is overcome, understanding America and the American way will come easier and be more genuine.

Vice-President Isidro of the University of the Philippines remarked as I left him: "Remember, the East has to know the East before it can engage effectively in East-West interchange." Hawaii can certainly be effective in both respects.

ence with, or even exposure to, any aspect of Asian studies, and there were more than a dozen professors who had the necessary expertise in this field. His reply was somewhat puzzling but understandable. He had called a conference of these Asian experts, especially those who successfully lobbied for this program in the legislature, to get some consensus on who should direct the new program. These scholars were somewhat narrowly specialized in their subject country areas of China, Japan, India, Russia, or Southeast Asia. There apparently was some feeling that all of them had some "ax to grind." Therefore, they decided to recommend someone completely neutral and an outsider and so they recommended me. I told the president to give me a few days to think over his proposition. After my own consultations with the interested faculty who pledged their support, I told the president I would accept the new appointment but under two conditions: First, I needed a two-month orientation trip throughout Asia to acquaint myself with people at the universities and education ministries with whom I would necessarily be working. This arrangement was a kind of "learning on the job." Second, my appointment was to be temporary while the University began looking for someone far better qualified for the job. This was a real left-handed appointment, but, as it turned out, it opened up many new doors for me.

My orientation trip to Asia was very extensive but, necessarily, somewhat superficial. Some impressions I got there were helpful to me later in running the program. In India I noted the abhorrence male university students felt toward any kind of manual labor. These students came from the upper classes and were accustomed to having servants do menial tasks. I also observed bathroom facilities that would never be tolerated in any dormitory in America. Bathrooms were left until the servants came to clean them, even if the filth festered for some time. In Malaya, Moslem students, the majority, refused to use the same cafeteria facilities as Chinese students because the dishes they used would be contaminated by pork. These kinds of cultural differences complicated many phases of university operations and had to be taken into consideration when running our own program at the University of Hawaii.

At the University of Burma in Rangoon, I learned some valuable lessons about making economic projections. Before I had left on this trip, I knew of a major economic study made by the Robert Nathans Associates of Washington, D.C., subsidized by the USAID. I also knew that this study proved to be a great disappointment and was no longer used. I wanted to find out from the native economists what went wrong. They were agreed that the misfortune of the study was based on two basic assumptions made at the very beginning of the study in order to make economic projections for the five following years. The first assumption had to do with weather conditions for the period. No one can scientifically forecast weather so they simply assumed that the weather conditions would continue as they had in the last five years. In an agriculture-based economy, the amount of rainfall is, of course, crucial, especially to their vital rice crop. Unfortunately, there was one of the driest seasons on record, and the weather projections were far off the target. The second assumption was even more confounding. It had to do with civil strife within the country. If the rebellion and fighting continued in the northern sector, it could adversely affect production, as it had in Vietnam and other destabilized economies in southeast Asia. On the assurance of Burma's defense department, it was assumed that the destabilizing factors would be neutralized. In actual fact, the situation got worse rather than better. With these two basic ill-founded assumptions, no projections could be of any value to the economic reconstruction of Burma in the post–World War II period.

In the U.S. we economists tend to ignore or underestimate cultural and religious barriers to economic development. We become frustrated and impatient with the sacred cows in India as they leisurely stroll or stall big trucks transporting industrial material and products on major thoroughfares. Even more frustrating is the sight of big, black crows picking up the seeds being sown by peasants in the countryside, completely immune to human harassment. In assessing economic problems in these underdeveloped areas, one has to be infinitely patient and understanding, even if exasperated.

The long and arduous trip through Asia would not have been possible without the help of the Asia Foundation. This private organization had offices and staff in every country I visited and provided me with all the logistical support I needed. More importantly, they made all the appointments for me. They were able to open doors I would have found most difficult or impossible. I later heard rumors to the effect that this organization was a front for, and run by, the CIA. To me, they were most helpful, and, to my knowledge, never tried to use me in any way.

The second condition I laid down in accepting the position of directing the Asian Studies Program was that a replacement should be found as soon as possible. My replacement was Dr. Ronald Anderson, who was a professor of comparative education at the University of Michigan. He was also the National Secretary of the Professional Association of Asian Studies and knew all the important people in the field well. Dr. Anderson was on temporary assignment at the University of Hawaii when I persuaded him to take over my job. It worked out well for all parties concerned.

East-West Center—1960

My assignment with the East-West Center was of short duration, just long enough for me to complete a trip through seventeen countries in Asia. The newly established Center needed to establish contacts in Asia and set up machinery for selection of students and scholars. The team of five sent by the University were the following: Dr. Baron Goto, Director, Hawaii Agricultural Extension Service; Dr. Thomas Ige, former Director, Asian Studies; Mr. William N. Wachter, Administrative Vice President, University of Hawaii; Dr. Kenneth Lau, Director, Legislative Reference Bureau, and Chairman, East-West Center Advisory Committee; and Dr. John N. Stalker, Director, Overseas Operations Program.

Countries visited were: Seoul, Korea; Naha, Okinawa; Tokyo, Japan; Taipei, Taiwan; Hong Kong; Manila, Philippines; Saigon, Vietnam; Vietiane, Laos; Phnom Penh, Cambodia; Bangkok, Thailand; Rangoon, Burma; Calcutta, India; Dacca, Pakistan; Katmandu, Nepal; New Delhi, India; Karachi, Pakistan; Madras, India; Colombo, Ceylon; Singapore;

East-West Center, *Left to right:* Dr. Baron Goto, Vice-President William Wachter, and Tom Ige

Djakarta, Indonesia; Sydney, Australia; Melbourne, Australia; and Wellington, New Zealand.

The long trip was exhausting but, in so many ways, very rewarding. The trip began on October 24th and lasted to December 14th. The American embassies or councils in all those countries made all the necessary appointments for us, as well as provided the logistical support. We were warmly welcomed wherever we went, and I felt we accomplished our mission to the fullest extent. For the first time the University of Hawaii had established working relationships with most of these Asian universities and the countries' ministries of education.

Assignments in Tokyo
Tachikawa Air Force Base—1975

During my University career, I had the good fortune to have two assignments in Tokyo, Japan. The first was actually an extension of the M.B.A. program of the College of Business

Administration at the Tachikawa Air Force Base outside of
Tokyo. Air force officers nearing retirement were eager and
highly motivated to take classes and get started on a career
after retirement from the air force. Most of the officers were
in their thirties and forties and proved to be far better than my
students on the Manoa campus. My schedule could not have
been made any easier. Two graduate seminars were held for
two-hour sessions on Tuesday and Thursday nights with
about twenty students in each session. I was provided with a
comfortable apartment on base with the equivalent of a GS 16
rating. The apartment was free and I received full pay from
the University with $300 a month extra for expenses. I never
had it so good! I enjoyed the commissary and officers' club
privileges, but the best part was the Showa golf course fifteen
minutes from the base, which I got to play quite often. Tachikawa has long had a reputation as a wild G.I. town and, to a
great extent, this was true. There were gaudy neon signs outside the drinking places with such names as "The Silver Sad-
dle," "Montana," and the "Golden Eagle." I enjoyed many an
evening with my students there. The assignment was for one
semester only and then another professor came to carry on.

Waseda University—1976

My second assignment was with Waseda University, a big and
prestigious university in Japan located in the Shinjuku area of
Tokyo. I taught two seminar-type courses there. Since few of
the students understood English, the classes were small,
about fifteen in each, so that we had ample opportunity to
exchange ideas. While I was there, there were student demonstrations, which I enjoyed watching. At the time, the big
demand was for the prosecution of Tokuyei Tanaka, the Japanese prime minister who resigned as a result of the Lockheed
scandal. Unlike our own Watergate case, prosecution in Japan
moved very slowly and quietly. I felt the students were fully
justified in clamoring for a faster resolution of the situation.
Tanaka, unlike Nixon at Watergate, still exercised full control
over the faction that controlled the ruling party.

I found the Japanese students very polite and eager to learn English. By their senior year most of the students had jobs already lined up with big corporations. Waseda, being a prestigious school especially in the business sector, had very strong connections and was able to place its graduates. In this respect, I think Japanese universities differ greatly from their American counterparts. I had always wondered why in Japan so much emphasis was placed on entering the "right" schools, where parents were willing to make enormous sacrifices and students committed suicide if they failed. Graduates from prestigious schools have automatic entry into lifetime jobs with companies having strong ties with particular universities. This kind of "in-breeding" also persists in the faculties of Japanese universities, where graduates from other universities are rarely considered for these positions. One rarely finds a professor shifting from one university to another, so common in America.

I recall with fond memories two incidents unrelated to my teaching at Waseda University. One had to do with the big Mitsui Bank. I helped found the City Bank in Honolulu and became one of its original directors. Mitsui Bank was our correspondent bank in Japan and acted as our "big brother." Whenever one of the directors, or top official, of City Bank in Honolulu visited Tokyo, Mitsui Bank was glad to be his host. When I visited Mitsui Bank, one of the grandsons of the founder was appointed to be my host and guide. One of the places he took me was the famous Yasukuni Shrine where the war heroes from generations past are enshrined. At the entrance was a small octagonal building on the face of which was depicted eight of the most glorious military victories from the past. One featured Admiral Heihachiro Togo smashing the Russian fleet during the Russo-Japanese War of 1904–1905. As we were admiring this plaque, I casually remarked to this grandson of the great Mitsui clan that my given Japanese name was Heihachiro. He looked at me and, with sincerity, said that I had a terrific name. I thought this amusing, coming from one of the most famous families in all Japan about a country boy from Kahaluu.

The other incident I recall during this stay in Japan had to do with a Hawaiian boy who was playing professional baseball in Japan at that time. His name was Wally Yonamine. The National League all-stars from the United States were in Japan for a series of games with the Japanese all-stars. The first game in Tokyo was sold out weeks in advance and tickets were not to be had. A friend of mine, a newspaper reporter, tried very hard to get tickets but to no avail. I was most anxious to see this game. In desperation, I finally got in touch with Wally who was on the Japanese all-star team. I had known Wally only casually in Hawaii through mutual friends, Toku Tanaka, Jimmy Asato, and others. He was most accommodating and, without any hesitation, told me to meet him at the main entrance of the Korakuen Stadium. When I went to the appointed place, Wally was patiently waiting with two tickets. After bowing to us, he rushed off to join his teammates warming up for the big game. Recalling this incident now, I feel ashamed for abusing this friendship. The Japanese news reporter who accompanied me was truly flabbergasted that the great Wally Yonamine who was the MVP and batting champion in previous years would be so humble and accommodating. The name Yonamine is a common Okinawan surname and my friend Roy Nakada, an attorney who practiced in Okinawa for decades, told me that Wally was long revered in Okinawa and they were most anxious to see him. Unfortunately, he never got to Okinawa during his glory years. As for the all-star game itself, the Americans were soundly beaten, much to the delight of Japanese fans. That night, about 2 A.M., I ran into Sad Sam Jones of the San Francisco Giants. He and some other American all-stars staggered out of a fancy nightclub in the Roppongi district. The National League officials stateside must have read them the riot act as the American all-stars played much better as the series progressed.

Consulting Work at University of Hawaii

Demand for the services of professional economists in the United States, as well as in Japan, is quite strong. Many university economists make more money outside than inside the university. I think this is even more true in Japan, where I found economics professors hard to locate on the campus of Waseda University. For me, this was no big deal. The largest task I took on in Hawaii was with the City Bank in 1958–1959. Obtaining a bank charter has always been the first big hurdle that organizers of a new bank in the community had to overcome. The "need" for a new bank in the community had to be clearly established. Along with Dr. Shelly Mark of our own Department of Economics of the University of Hawaii and Dr. Edwin Shaw of Stanford University, we spent many days in preparation, as well as presenting, our case before the bank examiners. We got it through without much difficulty.

In this joint study, I still recall the projections we made concerning the future economic growth of Hawaii. Dr. Shaw contended the projections Dr. Mark and I made were far too conservative. Since we were on the verge of obtaining statehood in 1959, Dr. Shaw contended that there was bound to be a vigorous surge in economic activity after statehood, as had happened in practically all new states. Therefore, he practically doubled our projected growth rates. In retrospect, he was correct and the actual growth of City Bank exceeded our expectations. The total assets now stand in the neighborhood of $400 million.

My other consulting projects were minor in nature. Among them was a mileage allowance study for the Hawaii Government Employees Association and work for Savings and Loan Associations. Perhaps my more important outside work was with the state legislature—analyzing the adequacy of our Unemployment Compensation Reserves, economic development on Maui, and so on.

Summer Exchanges

For a university professor the summer months are a time when you can choose what you want to do. One of the attractive alternatives for me was to spend the time at some other university. This helped to break the monotony of teaching at the same place year after year. I think this is also good for the university. It reinvigorates the professor and gives him some valuable new experiences and contacts. I had two of these temporary summer exchanges, one at Xavier University in Cincinnati, Ohio, and the other at my old school in Wisconsin.

I arranged an exchange with Dean Thomas Hailstone of the Business School of Xavier University through a mutual friend, Dr. K. K. Seo. Dean Hailstone always had a fondness for Hawaii, having taught a number of summers at Chaminade University in Honolulu. I had never been to Cincinnati or to the university there but I was open to new experiences and to meeting new people. I had always been a fan of the Cincinnati Reds, a formidable baseball team that dominated in the late seventies. The opportunity to see Johnny Bench, Tony Parez, Pete Rose, Joe Morgan, José Conception, and other stars play was an added attraction. I was not disappointed whenever I went to the Riverside Stadium to watch them play, and the enthusiasm of the fans was contagious. It was a kind of excitement one cannot experience watching the game on television.

The Hailstones and their children enjoyed our large home on Maunalani Heights which had a good swimming pool. Their house in an attractive suburb of Cincinnati was also big and very comfortable. My first night there, however, was most unfortunate and could have been tragic. After a long flight from Honolulu with one transfer, my wife and I arrived at the house at night, exhausted after many hours of flying. Unfamiliar with the house, I opened the wrong door trying to go upstairs to the bedroom and plunged to the basement cement floor in pitch darkness. My wife called an ambulance, and I spent three days in the hospital in a coma and missed the first week of class. Aside from this initial miss-step, the experience at the Hailstones' was most rewarding. In the Hailstones' brand new Buick, we leisurely toured the Ohio countryside and the Kentucky environs where Abraham Lincoln spent his early childhood. One can almost feel the presence of young Lincoln there. The famous horse-breeding farms around Lexington were also a treat to see. The night classes I held were no different from those in Hawaii.

Cincinnati, I read somewhere, was a city with some of the remnants of southern segregation, even on the baseball team. This kind of thing cannot be easily assessed, but I did sense some rigidity in the conservative social structure dominated by the power of the old-line Taft family.

The summer spent on the campus of the University of Wisconsin in Madison was more of a homecoming event for me. Having spent so many years there, it was like a second home. My wife and two children were spending the summer with her parents in nearby Minneapolis, so I repeated my bachelor days, staying at the University Club adjoining the campus. Renewing contacts with my former professors was refreshing. Being free all afternoon, however, gave me the rare privilege of golfing almost every day. Seiji Naya, now a key executive at the East-West Center in Hawaii but a graduate assistant at the University of Wisconsin at that time, was assigned to be my assistant for the summer. There was really nothing urgent for me or him to do, so we usually spent a pleasant afternoon at the many good golf courses in Madison. With all this leisure time, I never shot better golf than the summer I spent there.

CHAPTER 8

Invitation to Okinawa

Commencement Address

In late 1958 I received a letter from Dr. Asato, then president of the University of Ryukyu, to deliver the commencement address there the following March. This was indeed a most welcome honor. I understood that their university people were getting somewhat impatient with military generals and visiting American dignitaries addressing their graduating classes. As one of the first Americans of Okinawan descent to receive a Ph.D. in the United States, they wanted me to break tradition. The speech I made was as follows:

DR. THOMAS H. IGE

PROFESSOR OF ECONOMICS, UNIVERSITY OF HAWAII

TO

THE GRADUATING CLASS OF 1959

UNIVERSITY OF THE RYUKYUS

NEW HORIZONS IN A NEW AGE

THE SEVENTH ANNUAL COMMENCEMENT

March 2, 1959

I am very grateful for this opportunity to participate with you on this happy occasion of the Seventh Annual Commencement exercises of the University

Commencement address at the University of Ryukyu
(U.S.C.A.R. photo)

University of Ryukyu (U.S.C.A.R. photo)

of the Ryukyus. I wish to extend my hearty congrat-
ulations to each and every one of you graduates,
your parents, the University, and the Government
of the Ryukyu Islands, for making this kind of an
occasion possible. I have watched this ceremony,
not as a casual visitor and a guest speaker from
across the sea, but as one who was here and experienced the sufferings and anxieties through that
tragic summer of 1945. Out of the complete ruins,
chaos, and demoralization, together you have rebuilt a worthy civilization within a relatively short
period of time. This university, as well as the graduating class, represents to me proud symbols of your
great progress to date and the promise of a brighter
future.

   While you on Okinawa were busily engaged in the
tremendous task of rebuilding these islands, the
world outside has not stood still. The world today is
a vastly different world from the one which was
shaken at the time of Pearl Harbor. The Pacific and
Asian areas have come to occupy a more significant
role in the course of world events and will continue
to command more attention and respect from the
rest of the world. Added to this, we see the awesome
developments in science that virtually erase our old
concepts of space and distance. This is a new age full
of new meanings and responsibilities for all of us in
the Pacific area.

   As I speak before you today, Hawaii is on the
threshold of becoming the 50th State in the United
States of America. For the first time in the nearly
200 years of American history, a new state with a
population made up largely of people of oriental
descent will be admitted as a full partner in the
Union of States. United States Senator Henry M.
Jackson, Chairman of the Senate Insular Affairs
Committee, stated in Hawaii a few weeks ago that
Hawaii will not only be the 50th state but will
become the "Diplomatic State" to help bridge the

gap between the East and the West. This is clearly the kind of new thinking that is beginning to emerge with the coming of the new age—a new age where we at long last are coming to realize that true democracy and true brotherhood are not matters of the color of one's skin or the God one chooses to worship, but of the mind and of the heart. The horizons are slowly but surely lifting to reach beyond the narrow concepts of nationality and beyond the old political boundaries. In this new age of nuclear power and supersonic speed, this transformation of thinking is logical and absolutely necessary.

Before the start of World War II, Okinawa was practically unknown to the world outside of its neighboring areas. Today, almost 15 years after the war ended here, Okinawa is one of the few areas of the world equally prominent after the war as during the war. The world at large has long forgotten Bougainville, Guadalcanal, Saipan, and other scenes of bloody battles, but by virtue of geography, Okinawa—like Hawaii—has become destined to play a role far surpassing its size in the evolution of this new era in the Pacific. Like Hawaii, the land area as well as the population of Okinawa is small, but the role each plays can be catalytic and tremendously important symbolically.

With this new age of the Pacific Basin in mind, I note with great interest your recent conversion from the "B" Yen to the dollar. As an economist, I can see many advantages in this, not because the dollar is the American dollar, but because the dollar is the most generally accepted medium of exchange throughout the world today—just as the English sterling was a generation ago. Being the only area in the Far East with an economy based on the dollar, I can see great possibilities in terms of international monetary transactions and institutions. Added to this, I recently learned of your attempts to create a free trade zone on this island. This is an exciting

prospect! These two developments, as I see it, are
important steps which can help to bring about more
rapid economic development and the kind of international community and understanding that we so
desperately need.

You may say with Sakini of the "Teahouse of the
August Moon" that Okinawa has been dominated
by so many different peoples over the centuries that
you do not have the kind of spirit necessary to fulfill
your destiny in this new age. To me, the statue of
Kyuzo Toyama in Northern Okinawa is more symbolic of the true spirit of Okinawa than the "Teahouse" of escapism and self-indulgence. Mr.
Toyama's statement made a half century ago that
"your home is the five continents of the world"
stands truly prophetic today, as you emerge from
obscurity to help create a more international community in the Far East and the Pacific area. The
spirit of Toyama is the spirit of pioneers; it portrays
courage and vision to strike out boldly in new direc-
tions and new ventures. To the graduating students
and the young people in Okinawa generally, it is
very important to constantly bear in mind that you
are as capable of big things as the young people from
any other part of the world. This has been proven
time and again not only here on Okinawa but in all
parts of the world where people from these islands
have emigrated.

The world around us may drastically change, but
old loyalties and ideals which have stood for decades
change slowly and painfully. The role of the University of the Ryukyus is a crucial one. It must be the
major instrument in preparing the minds of the
young and the leaders of tomorrow to meet the challenge of this new age. The University is logically the
intellectual center of society. To the extent that this
University can provide the kind of leadership and
inspiration for the world of tomorrow, this society
will benefit and progress.

The University stands today where the castles
and shrines have stood for centuries in these beautiful hills of Shuri. I think this is symbolic of the new
age and role of the University in it. Castles and
shrines are sacred memories of the glories of the
past. The University looks to the future and trains
the leaders of the future. Of all the many activities
on this island today, military as well as civilian, I
see the functions of this University as the most
important over the long run. With true dedication
by the administration and the faculty, I am confident that you graduates of today and those to follow
will help to establish true internationalism in the
brave new world of tomorrow."

The United States Civil Administrations of the Ryukyu
Islands (USCAR) provided me with all the logistical support
on this trip; I traveled on a military plane with the equivalent
rank of a brigadier general. It was certainly a new experience
for a one-time army non-com. While the University officials
were waiting for me at the airport, I was quietly whisked away
from the plane in a big black VIP automobile. The University
people were later surprised and happy to see me since they
were sure I had missed the plane.

I was given an extra week in Okinawa to visit with relatives
and friends. The trip to Kin Village in northern Okinawa was
a sentimental journey. I had childhood memories of when I
attended the elementary school there for six months as a second grader. I was more than happy to give a short talk as the
school had requested, and I was flattered to learn they had a
big photograph of me hanging in the administration office.
During the Okinawan campaign, I had made a hasty visit to
Kin Village in the midst of their sufferings and general chaos.
This time the atmosphere there was calm and we were able to
laugh and reminisce over sake. On this trip my host was Seiho
Matsuoka, the chief executive of the islands for several years.
He was himself a native of Kin Village, and we had many rela-
tives in common.

On this visit to Okinawa I was also fortunate to renew my

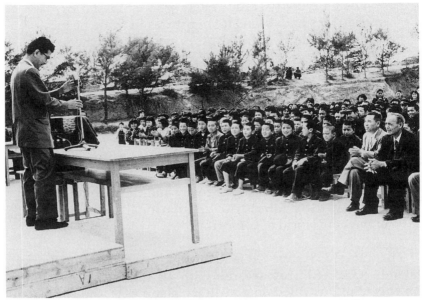

Speech given at Kin Elementary School, Okinawa (U.S.C.A.R. photo)

acquaintance with Ichiro Inamine, the wealthy owner of the Shell Oil franchise in the entire prefecture. He was a civic leader of note who pushed the development of new industries such as tea culture. He also headed the overseas emigration movement. A very charming, sophisticated leader, he was later voted into Japan's House of Peers, the equivalent of the U.S. Senate. Mr. Inamine was also a golfer, so we played a game at the Awase Meadows. During the course of the game, we discussed the future of economic development in Okinawa. He asked for my advice; one suggestion I made somewhat startled him. My suggestion was to develop golf courses to anchor a high-level tourist industry in Okinawa. In 1958 golf was still in its infancy in Japan and practically undeveloped in Okinawa. At that time, there were only two courses there—both U.S. military—one at Awase and another at the Kadena. When natives, like Inamine, had important guests from Japan who wanted to play golf they had to go, hat in hand, to get dispensation from the U.S. Army.

Golf as an essential ingredient in the tourist industry was

Tom with relatives in Kin Village (U.S.C.A.R. photo)

Left to right: Dad, Chief Executive Matsuoka, Tom, and two relatives at Kin Village (U.S.C.A.R. photo)

well recognized in the United States but in 1959 was not recognized in Japan or even in Hawaii. I told Inamine that Okinawa had certain natural features ideal for golf. Also, the cold winter months in Japan made the sun drenched islands of Okinawa a very desirable, convenient, and accessible retreat for tourists and golfers. Inamine became intrigued enough with this idea to take a day off to look at possible golf sites, especially on the west coast of the main island on the way to the northern city of Nago. We passed many picturesque little islands dotting the oceanside and sand beaches comparable to the best in Hawaii. We became quite excited about this golf fantasy which didn't begin to materialize until twenty years later. I certainly do not take credit for helping to motivate the development of golf courses in Okinawa, but I believe I was one of the first to appreciate the potential benefits of golf courses there.

One last observation on the American occupation and administration of the Ryukyu Islands. I had no qualms about the military needs of the U.S. presence there, having suffered through the bitter battles to wrest control from the Japanese. The civil administration, however, left much to be desired. I felt the U.S. Army, by its own nature, was ill-suited for the job of guiding a large civilian society. To begin with, the commanding general was the defacto governor with another subordinate general in charge of civil administration. These big "honchos" served only two years; thus, there was little coordination between the American administration of the Ryuku Islands and the Ryuku government. I noted an undercurrent of resentment and lack of sensitivity among the military leaders, especially in the lower echelons. Such signs as "No Okinawans and Dogs Allowed" on the best beaches reserved exclusively for Americans should not have been tolerated. The American administrators still operated on the premise that Japan was the enemy with very little attempt at consultation with native Okinawans. Everyone had to admit that even under the United Nations trusteeship agreement, reversion of the islands to Japan was just a question of time. The entire educational program for the native children, for example, should have been jointly programmed with the Japanese Ministry of Education instead of being unilaterally controlled by Americans who knew little about the Japanese educational system. Even the display of the Japanese flags in the schools was regarded as a lack of respect for the American occupation. The anti-American demonstrations of this period were started primarily because of a very natural desire, not only of the Okinawan students, but of labor unions and the populace at large to return to Japanese control. I believe this transition could have been handled more efficaciously.

Despite the shortcomings noted here, it must be conceded that the American occupation did a remarkable job of rebuilding the basic infrastructure of the Okinawan economy. By the time of reversion in 1972, I would say that, despite all the destruction of World War II, Okinawa was far better off than most prefectures of Japan itself.

CHAPTER 9

Off to Bolivia
1969

After serving six more years with the department and the University, my sabbatical year came up. I decided to do something which I thought would offer more than the usual adventure. I made plans to go to the jungles of Bolivia and Brazil in the headwaters of the Amazon River. One dares not venture into these far-off places without some justifiable purpose and assurance of assistance. My reason for taking this bold adventure was my concern for Okinawans overseas.

In the post–World War II rehabilitation of Okinawa the economic problems of overpopulation and underemployment became acute. Despite efforts by the United States, as U.N. trustee of the island, to raise the living standard of the islanders, physical and material limitations made the effort very difficult. As recovery began in Japan, many young people in Okinawa left for jobs in Japan, especially to the Osaka area. Jobs related to the military occupation were short-term at best and, in most cases, menial in nature. There was a revival of the spirit exemplified by Kyuzo Toyama at the turn of the century to "go abroad and seek a new home and future." Much of this focus was turned to South America as Okinawans had long emigrated and settled in Peru, Brazil, and Argentina. A report by Migoro Tamaki of the immigration section of the Agriculture and Forestry Department of the Government of Ryukyus entitled "Courses of Immigration Abroad from Okinawa Prefecture" gives the following facts and figures:

Peru. The first immigration into Peru from Okinawa started ed in 1906 when a group of 111 contract laborers were sent there. By 1938 their population had increased to over 11,000.

Brazil. The first immigrants into Brazil from Japan started when 168 families consisting of 781 persons arrived at Santos, Brazil, in June of 1908. As of September 1958, a total of 5,738 Okinawan families, with 41,735 persons, composed about 10% of the total Japanese-Brazilian population.

Argentina. Since 1913, 2,754 Okinawans had moved to Argentina. By 1948 Okinawan-Argentines started calling their relatives and in the post-war a total of 3,325 Okinawans had moved to Argentina.

Bolivia was to come much later and the first immigrants penetrated into Bolivia from Peru and Brazil following the rubber boom of the World War II period. By 1938, however, only 37 persons were recorded (vs. 11,311 for Peru).

Bolivia post-1950. Real efforts to send Okinawan immigrants to Bolivia began in the early 1950s, with the Japan-Bolivian agreement. Bolivia actively sought new immigrants to bolster its stagnating economy and offered many inducements to the Okinawan government. Dr. James L. Tigner of Stanford University was hired to do a feasibility study for the United States Civil Administration of the Ryukyu Islands (USCAR). His report concluded that Bolivia was an adequate region to which Okinawans could emigrate. Consequently, Uruma Immigration Association in Bolivia petitioned USCAR to send 3,000 family groups comprising some 12,000 persons annually. The petition was approved and the sum of $160,000 was budgeted for the first-year immigrants.

Under the leadership of Jugo Thoma, chief executive of the Ryukyu Government, and Ichiro Inamine, President of the Okinawan Overseas Association, large-scale immigration started in 1953.

The object of my journey into Bolivia, and to a lesser extent into Brazil, was to study what happened to these immigrants. Furthermore, my own first cousin and his family were involved in this emigration. After returning from my journey to Bolivia, I wrote a report in 1970 which was as follows:

Frontier Economics, The Bolivian Case

Land-scarce Japan with its heavy population pressures has long looked to the vast open spaces of

South America as a possible outlet for its people.
Over the past 60 years, the transpacific movement
of Japanese has resulted in the presence of over a
million South Americans of Japanese descent. In
Brazil alone an estimated 600,000 Brazilians with
Japanese blood account for more than twice the population of Japanese in the United States, including
Hawaii. (Much has been written in Japanese, Portuguese, and Spanish on the historical accounts of
the immigrants but very little can be found, especially in English, on the more recent status of these
people.)

I was in Bolivia in March, 1970. It attracted me
for it was here that the most recent major attempts
at "colonization" took place.

Bolivia is a small, land-locked country surrounded by Peru and Chile to the west, by Argentina
in the south and by Brazil to the east and north. Its
population of about four million has an average per
capita income of under $100 and its economy has
been based primarily on mining, especially tin in the
Andes mountains. The eastern half of Bolivia is a
low flood plain which forms part of the huge Amazon basin and is very fertile as well as sparsely popu-
lated. It is in this area, specifically in the province of
Santa Cruz, that the new Okinawan colonies have
settled in recent years.

Most observers, I believe, will label the economic
development of these colonies to date as "disappointing." Some may even say "grim." My major
observation is more optimistic, especially with
regard to future prospects.

Japanese immigration to Bolivia is a very recent
development. Prior to World War II immigrants into
Bolivia came indirectly through Peru when the rubber boom developed in the Amazon area during
World War I. In 1954 two organized colonies were
established in the Santa Cruz Province—one from
Okinawa and the other from Japan, mostly from the

Nagasaki area. The initial group from Okinawa consisted of 400, made up of 80 families and 80 single men. This group was government sponsored and heavily subsidized, including aid from the government of the Ryukyu Islands (¥million), the United States Civil Administration of Ryukyu (USCAR—$160,000), and by the local government of 350 million Bolivians. The Japanese colony was a private venture in the beginning but was taken over by the Japanese government at the request of the colonists after three years. This colony gradually built up to about 250 families with 1,500 people.

At the present time (1970) there are three Okinawan colonies. Colony No. 1, the oldest, has 209 families and 1,300 people; No. 2, established in 1959, now has 135 families with 793 inhabitants; and Colony No. 3, the most recent (1962), less than 50 families. No additional colonies from Japan proper were established in Bolivia since 1954.

The present "dark" side of the economic picture appears to be two-fold: (a) marketing and (b) production. Up to the present, all of these colonies concentrated on sugar and rice production. Until recently Bolivia has been a heavy importer of both commodities. In 1954, for example, she imported $4 million worth of sugar and more of rice. It was very logical that the new colonies select the site of their settlement as well as focus their production on these items. Within a few years these commodities were in surplus and prices fell sharply.

The marketing problem was further aggravated by price control and a very rudimentary form of production control. The politically conscious government of Bolivia aimed to keep the price of these basic commodities low even in the face of inflationary price increases in the rest of the economy. The political power rests in the mountainous mining regions in the Andes to the West. More than 80% of all consumer items are imported in Bolivia and prices of

these commodities have steadily risen year after
year while rice and sugar prices have been held sta-
ble and low. The Japanese (including Okinawan)
colonies, therefore, suffered more than proportionately from the economic effects of inflation.

The marketing problem worsened and became
almost hopeless this year when the revenues of the
Bolivian Government dropped sharply as a result of
the nationalization of the Gulf Oil Company (U.S.).
Not only is the price of rice, the major cash crop in
the colonies, controlled but the marketing is the
monopoly of the national government. You can sell
only to the government. This is also true in Japan
except the Japanese government buys at a price well
above what would be the free market price. In this
context it becomes exasperating to the rice growers
when the government says, "We can't buy as much
rice this year because our revenue is down." Royal-
ties from oil were running over six million dollars a
year. With the takeover, oil export has dropped to
zero and the fiscal condition of the national government has become very shaky. The dilemma was
graphically visible in the cooperative marketing
center of the Okinawan colonies as last year's crop
was coming in while parts of the previous year's
harvest still remained unsold in the warehouse—
decreasing in value as the months went by.

The production problem is also a dilemma, with
overproduction on the one hand and underproduction on the other. For the agricultural sector of the
Bolivian economy as a whole, production of basic
agricultural commodities like rice and sugar
increased more than a 100% since these colonies
moved in. This was partly due to their efforts. The
shift from import to export of these basic commodities was the result of drastically improved "infrastructure" in Bolivia over the same period. At this
stage of their economic development "infrastructure" meant good roads. The establishment of the

original colonies in 1954 coincided with the completion of the first paved highway between the city of Santa Cruz, the capital and economic center of the vast flood plains in the Amazon region of Bolivia, and with the major population centers of the mountainous mining regions where 80% of the population lives. The opening of this vital highway was only the beginning of other paved roads into the vast lowlands of the counties. Native colonies mushroomed all along these new roads with little or no government help of any kind. It was the stated objective of Bolivia's new economic policy to relocate at least a half-a-million people to the fertile, little exploited lowlands, especially in Santa Cruz province. This tidal wave of new immigrants to the agricultural sector boosted production far beyond what the new Japanese and Okinawan colonies could add. At its peak, these colonies accounted for more than 30% of all rice produced in Bolivia; later it was about 5% of the greatly increased overall production. The colonists complain of the "small" Bolivian market despite new roads and access to the markets in the highlands.

Another aspect of the production dilemma is underproduction within the Okinawan colonies. The Japanese colony in San Juan never had this problem. The site was specifically and scientifically selected for rice growing and its productivity in rice was, without doubt, the highest in the country. In addition, the Japanese colony has had the expert guidance of a permanent agricultural experiment station subsidized by the Japanese government and headed by a genial dynamo named Hirano over the last ten years. Production problems, on the other hand, have plagued the Okinawan colonies from the very beginning. It appears that the sites selected along the Rio Grande River were poorly suited for rice and sugar cane cultivation. The rainfall in this region was, on the average, less than half that of the

Japanese colony to the west along the foothills of the
Andes. There is no "suito" or wet, paddy-style rice
growing; therefore, rain at the right time was very
crucial to the kind of harvest a farmer got. This year
(1969), for the second consecutive year, insufficient
rains in the Okinawan colonies yielded a harvest
30–50% of normal output. The growers maintain
that it's a gamble with the weather where the odds
are generally 2 to 1 against you.

It seems contradictory to state that floods of drastic proportions also plague the Okinawan colonies.
Heavy rains in the surrounding mountains hundreds
of miles away flow into the Rio Grande and flood
the river banks for miles, even when rainfall in the
farmlands of the colonists may be low. The latest
overflow of the Rio Grande severely inundated about
a third of the rice farms and caused many to throw
up their hands in despair. The Japanese colony
located on higher elevation where flooding was no
major problem.

What then of the future? Is there any hope for
these pioneers who have courageously endured
untold hardship in these deep jungles of the Amazon? I am optimistic. By and large, most of the settlers are also optimistic and morale remains amaz-
ingly high. Even more interesting is the fact that
there appeared to be greater enthusiasm in the
Okinawan colonies which have suffered so many
setbacks than in the more prosperous Japanese colony about 200 miles west of the Okinawan colonies.

The spirit of optimism, as I see it, is based on at
least three grounds: (1) The systematic switch to
cattle ranching, (2) The steady increase in the value
of bigger and bigger land holdings by the settlers,
and (3) The vigorous population and industrial
growth of the Santa Cruz area.

Sugar and rice are dead. This was a general consensus in all the colonies. In the three Okinawan
colonies the transition is rapidly under way to cattle

ranching. The big word everywhere was "boku jo"—
cattle ranching. The Japanese colony at San Juan is
floundering badly as "boku jo" is not well suited to
their "wet" climate. They must, for the time being,
continue their rice production at which they are
most proficient and experiment with other crops. It
seems ironic that the sites of the Okinawan colonies
chosen for rice production turned out bad for rice
but excellent for cattle raising.

In the Okinawan colonies today the progress of a
settler is measured in terms of the number of head of
cattle he has and the acres planted to "boku cho"—
cattle grass, which must be fenced in. There was
real enthusiasm in this and everybody seemed to
know how many head of cattle every other farmer
had. Colony No. 2 may be taken as more typical
than No. 1. Among the 135 families they had over
1,500 head which averaged about 11 for each family
—with the grassed and fenced pasture land running
close to a hundred acres each. This average, however, is misleading as the more progressive settlers
had over 200 head of cattle and 500 acres of fenced-
in land. The goal of each rancher was to double his
herd and pasturage each year. One can already see
the emergence of the genuine "Okinawan cowboy"
in the jungles of Bolivia.

What about the economics of this new industry?
What assurance is there that the market may not
drop out from under them again?

First, on the production side, a switch to cattle
ranching is an expensive proposition. How can the
farmers afford this? It is estimated that one acre of
pasturage will support one cow, and one must have
at least 200 head at any one time to become a full-
fledged rancher.

The heavy investments made to date in clearing
the thick jungles for rice and sugar can now be easily
planted in cattle grass. Each farmer was given, for
free, 50 hectares (or 125 acres) to begin with and

most farmers have cleared at least half their holdings. The "Servicio de Immigracion" run by the Foreign Affairs Ministry of the Japanese government
has a field office in Colony No. 1 and is quite liberal
with its loans to farmers. To a great extent, this
office sets the tone for the farmers. It was set up following a visit by Mr. Seiho Matsuoka, then Chief
Executive of the Government of the Ryukyu Islands
Most of the "seed" money originated here and the
extent to which the agents from this office went out
and tried to help the settlers was truly admirable.
Mr. Sakae Kishikawa, in charge for the last two
years, was probably more responsible than anybody
else for the new turn and new hope in the Okinawan
colonies. "Reversion of Okinawa to Japan" is not
something that's going to happen; in Bolivia, for all
practical purposes, this has already happened.

Young calves can be bought for $30–$50 and in
a little over a year sold for $150–$200 on the hoof
at the farm. Buyers are constantly coming to the
farms, and cattle raised in the colonies are getting a
good reputation for quality. Corn is easy to grow and
corn fields are replacing the sugar cane as the march
to "Boku jo" accelerates each year. "No one has yet
lost any money on cattle" was a standard observation.

The really sad story in the Okinawan colonies is
the number of families which gave up and left. In
Colony No. 2, for example, there were 230 families
at one time; now it's down to 135—over 40% have
abandoned their hopes. For those who remained,
however, the transition to cattle raising was made
easier by the acquisition of additional lands from
those who left. The average price, I understand, was
about $500 for the standard 125 acres, much of it
already cleared.

Will cattle raising go the same way as sugar and
rice? I don't think so. Even in the United States
sugar and rice had been in oversupply for nearly 40

years, but meat, no. Per capita consumption of meat goes up steadily and more than proportionately with increases in incomes. Even in Japan, consumption of meat, per capita, has almost doubled over the past decade. The income elasticity of meat consumption is very high, and low for sugar and rice. This principle of consumer economics holds true worldwide. This meat-scarce country of Bolivia has been and will continue to be supplied from nearby Argentina and Brazil. In the meantime, she can absorb all meat produced at home for a long, long time.

The second basis for optimism is the rapid increase in land values. In a frontier economy, land values are determined to a great extent by accessibility. There is practically no value to fertile land located hundreds of miles away in areas where there is no means of transportation. This kind of land is still available for free and initially this is what the colonists got. As roads were built or improved the value of land went up correspondingly. Since the colonies were established beginning in 1954 more roads have been built in Santa Cruz Province during that short period of time than in the previous hundred years. The major highway between Santa Cruz and Montero, the nearest city from the colonies, has been paved and widened. You can now drive sixty miles an hour with no trouble. From Montero to San Juan to the west and Colony No. 1 to the east, roads have also been paved over the last few years. When one remembers that it was only a little over ten years ago that the original settlers in Colony No. 1 hacked their way through jungle swamps to get to their site, the progress is startling. Where it took three days to make a trip to Santa Cruz City, it could now be made in three hours with comfort. The value of all land along these major highways has more than doubled during the last five years and new economic activities could be seen sprouting everywhere.

Less than half a year ago the United States provided aid funds to complete the interconnecting roads between Colonies 1, 2, and 3. These were unpaved but were all-weather roads. Up to last November (1969) the only "road" connecting the colonies was a narrow clearing improvised by the colonists themselves and impassable much of the time. The opening of the new road which runs over a hundred miles was a milestone and immediately enhanced property values in the entire region.

The latest and even more significant improvement in roads was being undertaken with funds and equipment provided by the Japanese government. They just completed a big road improvement program within the Japanese colony at San Juan and moved the equipment to the Okinawan colonies. Another million dollars was budgeted over the next five years and this program will bring the all-weather road right up to the property of each and every settler. This may sound improbable at first but the layout of properties within each colony made this feasible. The 125-acre plots are neatly staked out in rectangles like the pineapple fields in the flatlands of Wahiawa, Hawaii. The plan was to improve every other road now in use thus ensuring good access to all settlers. When the project was completed, the heavy equipment was donated to the settlers to enable adequate maintenance of these roads.

With the completion of each phase of the road-building program, property values increased sharply. Even though one has no intention of selling his land holdings, the added value is a very tangible, usable thing. Instead of spending ten hours trying to get to the main highway from Colony 2, you get there in one hour now and the "frontier" becomes less foreboding and more attractive.

If one were to ask about the economic status of an average settler I would certainly not use the standard measure of "per capita or family income." At this stage "wealth" or "assets" would be a more appropriate measure of the economic progress. In terms of the standard per capita income, I would estimate this to be around $250 with the average running higher in the older Colony No. 1 and lower in the newest colony. At San Juan the corresponding figure may exceed $400 and come close to that of rural Japan. The average settler is more concerned with building up his assets at this stage. When 25 acres of jungle land is cleared this does not add to income but does enhance his assets; likewise, fencing his pastures and putting in a new well also enhances assets. Over the long run, it is these assets which will permit him a comfortable standard of living. In terms of assets, then, the settlers are doing very well which compares more than favorably with their counterparts in Japan or Okinawa.

The last but more basic reason for my optimism is the rapid economic development of the Santa Cruz area. In all of Bolivia it is the only province with a "boom" atmosphere. The population has doubled in ten years and is likely to accelerate. All this is not accidental as national economic policy is specifically aimed at development of the interior. This policy coincides with the observations of the multinational Economic Development Bank, the Alliance for Progress and the United Nations Economic Commissioner for Latin America. They all urge Bolivia to look to its lowland frontier for its economic salvation. The long-neglected frontier is beginning to bloom and the resources here are almost limitless. Large reserves of oil were discovered in the immediate neighborhood of the Japanese colony of San Juan. New people and new industries are constantly moving in. Even in the area around Okinawa Colony No. 3 while the number of colonists were decreasing the Mennonites from Canada have practically surrounded this colony and increased its own settle-

ment more than two-fold to 250 families. This is
more typical when one looks at the entire region—
people are not leaving but flooding into this area.
The city of Santa Cruz was a sleepy town of 40,000
and lay stagnant for a hundred years. Since 1954 its
population zoomed to nearly a hundred thousand.
Only four automobiles were seen in the muddy
streets of this city when the settlers first came. Now
traffic signals guard each major intersection as hundreds of Japanese-made cars and trucks ride the
newly paved streets of this booming city.

The dark days of the colonists here are definitely
over. They have suffered much and hardly anyone
has made it big yet. Solid foundations are being built
to take advantage of a rapid economic growth that is
already underway. In the meantime, no one is starv-
ing. Ducks, chickens, pigs, grapefruit, rice, and corn
are plentiful right on the farm. The problem from
now on is "making money" and I have a definite
feeling the colonists are riding with the wave of the
future Bolivia.

I had a feeling of sadness as I left the Okinawan colonies in
Bolivia. Basically, I felt that they were going through what
our own parents went through in Kahaluu in the nineteen-
twenties. My own cousin's home in Colony No. 2 may have
been typical. I was invited to a dinner party there with neighbors in the same area. Chickens were roasted on the outdoor
barbecue and we had a wonderful time. In the meantime,
however, I was overwhelmed by mosquitoes and other insects. I thought I was adequately clothed but upon returning
to my hotel in the city of Santa Cruz, my arms and legs were
badly swollen. I had a bottle of Johnny Walker so I sacrificed it
to drench several hotel towels in order to rub my sores. The
next day the hotel maid was very angry at me for ruining her
towels thinking I had a drunken spree. Upon seeing my badly
swollen legs and arms, she sympathized with me after accepting payment for damaging her towels. When one thinks of the
jungles of the Amazon, we usually picture the potential dan-

gers from all kinds of wild animals, snakes, piranha, wild Indians and so on, but I found the little insects most frightening. They told me a white horse can turn black at night when mosquitoes and insects cover it.

The kitchen floor in my cousin's home was made of hardened dirt; the kitchen had very little in the way of appliances. Majestic trees were still growing on his allotted acres, most of which were recently cleared. He told me he used native Indians for the hard labor involved. Despite his valiant efforts, he finally gave up a few years later to return to Okinawa when the economic boom there materialized with the preparation of the big world ocean exposition of the mid-seventies.

While traveling through the colonies, I slept at a crude guest house in Colony No. 1 but had to make-do in the small infirmaries in Colonies No. 2 and 3. Upon returning to Hawaii I came down with tuberculosis within six months with a half-year of hospitalization to follow.

On to Brazil

The major concentration of Okinawans outside of Sao Paulo on the metropolitan Atlantic coast area was in the frontier city of Campo Grande in the vast Mato Grasso province far off to the west, bordering Bolivia. Though only about five hundred miles from Santa Cruz in Bolivia, there were no transportation facilities so I decided to go the long way—visiting Buenos Aires in Argentina where the Okinawans, I was told, did very well in the service industries, especially in the flower and laundry businesses. Sao Paulo, Brazil reminded me of Los Angeles where Japanese were well entrenched in all facets of its society including representation in their national parliament.

The city of Campo Grande on the western edge of Brazil reminded me of American frontier towns like Dodge City, Kansas or Abilene, Texas when our own pioneers were pushing west and north. Campo Grande was covered with branches of the big banks of Sao Paulo and Rio De Janeiro, anxious to finance new ventures into the wilderness. It had a boom town

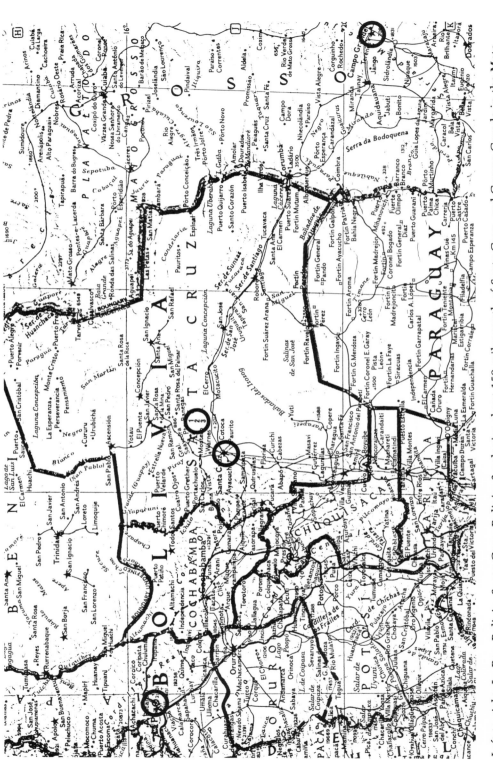

Left to right: La Paz, Bolivia; Santa Cruz, Bolivia; 3 colonies about 150 miles north of Santa Cruz; and Campo Grande in the Mato Grosso province of Brazil

atmosphere when I visited there. I was most amused to watch Indians brought from the wild to work on construction projects on a short-term basis. I was told that they liked Chinese cooking and I watched while they ate without the benefit of chop sticks.

The Okinawans at Campo Grande seemed far better off and settled than in Bolivia. There were no colonies but mostly individual enterprises on farms and small businesses. The produce business, in particular, seemed to be controlled by Okinawans and I enjoyed watching activities around the various stalls in a big market place. I was proud of the advancements made here and hoped that Okinawans in Bolivia would reach the same degree of affluence found in Campo Grande, Brazil.

CHAPTER 10

Off to Washington, D.C. 1963–1964

With Senator Inouye

In early December 1962 I received a telephone call from Daniel K. Inouye, who had just been elected to the U.S. Senate after serving two years in the House of Representatives. He asked me if I would become his administrative assistant in Washington, D.C. I was surprised and flattered by his offer. I had always supported him in his various campaigns, but I had never been very close to him at any time. He explained that the administrative assistant position would be his top staff aide. Although I had only a vague idea what my duties would entail, I felt it offered me the kind of experience I could never hope to get elsewhere.

The University was most willing to accommodate the Senator since I could then be of help on University matters along with my other duties. I received a two-year leave of absence. I left for Washington before the beginning of the second semester in February 1963. Because of such short notice I left my family behind; Fumi was working at Lewers and Cooke and my two children were both in the middle of their school year at Punahou. I found temporary lodging at the Carrol Arms Hotel across the street from the Senate office building. Staying there with me was Henry Guigni, the Senator's long-time aide and confidant who later became the Senate's sergeant at arms, one of the most powerful jobs on the Hill.

The new assignment proved very disappointing in many respects but most rewarding in others. Perhaps the major cause of my unhappiness was that my expectations were too

Dr. Thomas H. Ige, Administrative Aide: Professor Ige, economics department chairman, will be Inouye's administrative assistant. His duties will include attending senate committee hearings, and investigating various requests from Hawaii constituents, the University, and public organizations.

Senator Daniel K. Inouye. (*Honolulu Star-Bulletin* photo)

high and somewhat fanciful. As a professional economist with a wide range of experience, I had hoped to help the Senator in his deliberations on various major legislation and perhaps to substitute for him in some of his many committee assignments. The job, however, turned out to be what might be termed a flunkie job!

The Senator's office, like those of all senators, received hundreds of letters every week. The primary duty of the staff was to respond to these letters. Since most of these were from his constituents, it was very important for the Senator to give high priority to answering them. Only a very few of these letters were important enough to deserve the full attention of a busy senator, so it was up to the staff to respond as best they could. The final replies, of course, would be checked by the Senator and would be sent out under his signature.

Most of these requests were for the Senator's help or advice or were personal, and, in many cases, they were very petty in nature. I'm sure the parties writing these letters felt their problems deserved the Senator's time and attention. Some of these dealt with administrative decisions by some federal agency such as the Social Security Administration, the U.S. Army, Navy, Air Force, the Veterans Administration, any one of the bureaucracies surrounding the operations of the U.S. government. I remember with amusement one particular letter from a well-known lady in Honolulu, who wrote to protest the waste of federal funds in keeping the flame lit on the gravesite of former President John F. Kennedy which burned continuously at the Arlington Cemetery. I can't remember how I responded, but it was exasperating at best.

As a professional economist, I began to feel that I was wasting my time on these menial assignments and felt the urge to return to my duties at the University before the end of my two-year leave. After a year and a half, I left for home.

The Senator himself was most gracious at all times and I was very impressed with his performance in the U.S. Senate. I had the privilege of standing in the back of the Senate chamber to listen to his maiden speech in which he defended the rights of small states even if a filibuster was required. It was generally agreed that his pronunciation and enunciation of the English language were rarely matched in the Senate. His style of delivery was also captivating, low-keyed but powerful. Senator Inouye was highly respected by his colleagues; he was never aggressive and he knew when and where to accommodate. It is easy to see now how he built his power base in the Senate.

Civil Rights

While working for the Senator, I was able to enjoy many fringe benefits. The one I will never forget was participating in the great "March on Washington" in the summer of 1963. Actually I did not march along with the civil rights activists, but I substituted for the Senator who had to preside in the Senate that day. Along with other dignitaries, I rode in a special bus to the Lincoln Memorial. There on the steps, just behind the speakers' rostrum, I sat with other senators and leaders of the movement. The speech by the Reverend Martin Luther King that day will remain forever as one of the greatest in American history. I quote here part of that memorable speech:

> We cannot be satisfied so long as the Negro in Mississippi cannot vote and the Negro in New York believes he has nothing for which to vote. No, no, we will not be satisfied until justice rolls down like water and righteousness like a mighty stream.
> I am not unmindful that some of you have come here out of great trials and tribulations. Some of you have come from narrow jail cells. Some of you have come from areas where your quest for freedom left you battered by the storms of persecution and staggered by the winds of police brutality. You have been the veterans of creative suffering. Continue to work with the faith that unearned suffering is redemptive.
> Go back to Mississippi. Go back to Alabama; go back to South Carolina; go back to Georgia; go back to Louisiana; go back to the slums and ghettoes of our northern cities knowing that somehow this situ

Senators and others on the steps in front of the Lincoln Memorial in the "March on Washington," in the summer 1963

ation can and will be changed. Let us not wallow in the valley of despair.

I say to you today, my friends, even though we face the difficulties of today and tomorrow, I still have a dream. It is a dream deeply rooted in the American dream. I have a dream that one day this Nation will rise up and live out the true meaning of its creeds—"we hold these truths to be self-evident that all men are created equal."

I have a dream that one day on the red hills of Georgia the sons of slaves and the sons of former slaveowners will be able to sit down together at the table of brotherhood. I have a dream that one day even the state of Mississippi, sweltering with the heat of injustice, sweltering with the heat of oppression, will be transformed into an oasis of freedom and justice.

I have a dream that my four little children will one day live in a Nation where they will not be judged by the color of their skins, but by the conduct of their character.

I have a dream that one day in Alabama, with this vicious racist, its Governor, having his lips dripping the words of interposition and nullification—one day right there in Alabama, little black boys and black girls will be able to join hands with little white boys and little white girls as brothers and sisters.

I have a dream that one day every valley shall be exalted: every hill and mountain shall be made low, the rough places will be made plane, the crooked places will be made straight and the glory of the Lord shall be revealed and all flesh shall see it together.

This is our hope. This is the faith that I go back to the South with. With this faith, we will be able to hew out of the mountains of despair a stone of hope. With this faith, we will be able to transform the jangling discord of our Nation into a beautiful symphony of brotherhood. With this faith, we will be able to work together; to play together; to struggle together; to go to jail together; to stand up for freedom together knowing that we will be free one day. . . ."

Being right there, facing thousands of supporters around the reflecting pool between Lincoln Memorial and the Washington Monument, was perhaps the most moving experience of my whole life.

The funeral for the late President John F. Kennedy was another experience I will never forget. I was in the Senate barbershop when the first news flashes of the tragedy broke. We were almost in panic as the news was fragmented and sometimes contradictory. As it was first reported, there was wide speculation that the assassination was perpetrated by the extreme right fanatics of Dallas. We were not sure whether the President was dead or only seriously wounded. You can well imagine the pandemonium. The funeral that followed later began from the national Capitol building; it was somber but very majestic. The most touching moment for me was to watch the President's little son, John-John, haltingly salute his father as the caisson went slowly by.

U.S. Open

On a happier note, I was able to take in the U.S. Open golf tournament that was held at the Congressional Country Club just outside the Washington city limits in Maryland. This was during the summer of 1963. My buddy Jimmy Asato, the football coach at the University of Hawaii, and Ed Toma, then Athletic Director at McKinley High School, were in town to do some recruiting after attending a conference in New York. With my wife, I took them to the tournament. We followed Ted Makalena for the first few holes, the only Hawaiian boy in the professional tour then. We were delighted to see him outdrive the more famous players on the tour, but he was not among the leaders. It was one of the hottest days in the Washington area and since the third round on Saturday was washed out, the fourth round on Sunday was for thirty-six holes of play. It got so hot and uncomfortable that we decided to go to the final hole and sit in the shade.

Toward the end of the tournament we watched the final foursome coming in. In contention was Ken Venturi, who was so exhausted and dehydrated that a doctor had to accompany him as he staggered toward the final hole—a par five. His third shot landed in a sand trap right in front of where we were sitting. He was so weakened that he barely made it to the sand trap. The green sloped to a lake on the far side. One misplay here would have cost him the most prestigious prize in golf. Wobbly but determined, he neatly blasted onto the green and two-putted for the coveted prize. I have never witnessed a gutsier display of courage and skill under the most trying circumstances. Whenever I see Ken Venturi commentating on TV now, I recall his biggest triumph that day at the Congressional Country Club.

Junket

Often times one reads of trips by congressmen and/or staff referred to disparagingly as "junkets." Substituting for my senator, the one trip I remember was to inspect our naval base at Guantanamo, Cuba. The aircraft we took was the "Sacred Cow" which was once used by President Harry S. Truman as his official plane. It was luxuriously fitted and serviced by navy personnel. We had extravagant food and drinks all the way to Cuba. For a country boy from Kahaluu, this kind of accommodation and treatment was beyond imagination.

I never knew why this trip was arranged or what benefits were to be derived from it, but, as the saying goes, "never look a gift horse in the mouth." We enjoyed the hospitality and we were made to feel very important. In navy helicopters we leisurely flew over the entire base as well as the surrounding mountain areas of Cuban territory. The barbed wire fence enclosing the base was a very skimpy affair and Cuban soldiers could be seen on the other side behaving with complete abandon in spite of the American presence. The thing that impressed me most was the degree of cooperation that actually existed with this supposedly unfriendly country. For example, most of the fresh water supply to the base came from the Cuban side and could be shut off at any time. This was similar to Red China providing water for Hong Kong.

We went to the main gate of the base where thousands of Cubans entered and exited each day to work on various jobs. The security checks seemed no tighter than for civilian workers entering Pearl Harbor. The base, however, was heavily fortified with a strong presence of naval power—a comforting sight for us to observe.

Mexico

On the way home to Hawaii from Washington, D.C., our family decided to take a leisurely journey through the southland into Mexico. Through the Appalachian mountains we went through Knoxville and Chattanooga, Tennessee into Alabama and Mississippi to New Orleans. There we got a taste of the

night life in this exciting city. Leaving New Orleans, I wanted
to see some of the handiwork of the infamous Huey Long, so
we went to Baton Rouge to marvel at the beautiful buildings
of Louisiana State University and the state capitol. After we
left Louisiana, we motored through Houston and San Antonio
to cross into Mexico at Laredo on the Rio Grande.

From the northern city of Monterrey we motored south
through the mountainous parts of central Mexico. One can
easily see the poverty of rural Mexico where small farmers
planted corn so far into the mountains that they could barely
stand or walk. On the flat low lands were prosperous-looking
large estates, almost like plantations. On this mountainous
route we lost two new tires. My family's hotel accommodations were of the most primitive kind, so much so that my
wife and daughter chose to sleep in the car on some nights.

Driving late at night into Mexico City, we had difficulty
getting rooms at a hotel. In desperation, we tried the Ramada
Hotel, the best and most expensive in Mexico City. The only
rooms remaining were suites reserved for VIPs. We had no
choice but to pay a price we couldn't afford. For one night we
luxuriated before moving to a less expensive hotel to make up
for the hardships endured on the road.

Further south—almost to Guatemala—we enjoyed our stay
at the ancient city of Oaxaca. Here we got the feel of the real
Mexico. The open markets there were something to behold
with their genuine native crafts and products in full display.
The remnants of the early Mayan civilization could also be
seen more readily in this area.

On the way back to the States, we passed through Guadala-
jara, a truly delightful city, then went on to Mazatlan for a
banquet of all kinds of seafood. For the next five hundred
miles to the border at Nogales, Arizona, we traveled mostly
through small towns crowded in by very dry mountain ranges
of the Sierra Madre Occidental. The roads were so bad we lost
two more tires. Crossing into Arizona and then into Tucson
was a great relief though our sojourn through Mexico proved
exciting and certainly very educational.

CHAPTER 11

Back to Hawaii
1965–1970

Political Warfare

I have been a lifelong Democrat. How this happened I'm not sure. I grew up during the depression years of the early thirties, and Franklin Delano Roosevelt and the New Deal had a tremendous impact on my thinking. These were years of great economic hardships, but they were also very exciting with the National Industrial Recovery Act (NRA), the WPA, the FERA, NYA, CCC, AAA, and other agencies trying desperately to get the nation out of an ever deepening doldrum. I recall that even as a student in high school and college I was very sensitive and concerned about the political turmoil of the period, as were my classmates.

The Republican dominance of politics in Hawaii during the thirties left the Democrats with little to offer the young. The governor of the territory was appointed by the President and we had no representation in Congress. The highest elected official, therefore, was the non-voting delegate to Congress. Very few of the students at the University were actively engaged in partisan politics. During this period, however, I began developing what may be termed a "liberal" political philosophy that embraced the New Deal. This coincided with the awakening of the new labor movement in Hawaii.

During the first waterfront strike of the late thirties I helped provide the strike kitchen on the north or *ewa* side of River Street with produce from the country. Intellectually, I found the leadership of the Reverend Galen Weaver of the Church of the Crossroads very stimulating. Without doubt, he was the most liberal and outspoken clergy of the period. My favorite reading materials were the *New Republic* and *The Nation* magazines. The University faculty, by and large, were apolitical though a few professors like Dr. William Taylor and Dr. Harold Hoflick seemed quite sympathetic to the New Deal.

It was not until I started to teach at the University of Minnesota in the late forties that I started to actively participate in partisan politics. This was in the first campaign of Hubert H. Humphrey for the U.S. Senate. He had already served with distinction as mayor of the city of Minneapolis and we won quite handily. Later in Virginia my wife and I campaigned for Adlai Stevenson in his bid for the presidency. This was a failure, though he was a great inspiration to us.

I returned to Hawaii in 1953 and joined the faculty of the University of Hawaii. It seemed only natural that I take up with the young Democrats of the post-war period, who were seriously challenging the long-established political power structure in Hawaii. Under the leadership of Jack Burns, the returning Nisei war veterans joined with the newly invigorated labor unions to form the backbone of the new Democratic Party in Hawaii. I enthusiastically supported the "revolution" of 1954, when the party finally took political control after decades of docile accommodation. I strongly supported Jack Burns in his race for the delegate's seat in Congress. After statehood, I campaigned for him again in paid ads and television in his unsuccessful and later successful race for the governorship of our new state.

Campaign of 1966 for Lieutenant Governor

The campaign in 1966 and the following one in 1970 were, without doubt, the bitterest in the history of the Democratic Party in Hawaii. They were actually the culmination of the long-running feud between Jack Burns and his establishment on one side and Thomas P. Gill, the young challenger just returned from serving one term in the U.S. House of Representatives, on the other. As a leader in the state legislature, Gill was a big part of the political and social revolution.

Philosophically, I did not see too much difference between the two. Both might have been termed liberal democrats. Burns' support came from the Americans of Japanese Ancestry (AJA) and the labor unions headed by the International Longshoremen and Warehousemen Union (ILWU). The incumbency of the governor provided ample access to financial support from the business community, especially in the construction industry. Technically, the contest for Lieutenant Governor in 1966 was between Tom Gill and Kenneth Brown, who was anointed by Burns to take the baton for the Burns establishment. The choice of Brown was a big surprise to most Democrats, for he was never active in the affairs of the party. Some even suspected that he was a Republican. It was somewhat like the choice of Dan Quayle by Vice President George Bush at New Orleans in the summer of 1988—a real surprise.

In June 1966 I received a call from Tom Gill to be chairman of his campaign. This came as a complete surprise to me because the campaign was already underway and I was not a part of his inner circle of strategists. At the time I was the director of the Economic Research Center at the University and was reluctant to assume additional responsibilities, but I consented to help him as best I could. I came to know Tom Gill at close range while serving with Senator Dan Inouye in Washington in 1963 and part of 1964. At that time, Tom Gill was elected to serve in the U.S. House of Representatives. In his brief, one-term stint in Congress, he made a very favorable impression as a "comer" and was assigned to monitor an important section of the Civil Rights Bill, the most crucial legislation of the session. He was the only freshman congressman so honored, and he carried out his duties with distinction. I saw in him the potential of a national leader and became a staunch supporter.

No more than a few days after my choice to serve as Gill's campaign manager was announced in the press, I received a call from Governor John A. Burns. He was very unhappy with my decision and did not mince words as he castigated me. I told him that we were not running against him but against the unknown newcomer, Kenneth Brown. He did not accept my explanation and insisted that he personally was being chal-

John Burns and Tom Gill campaigning, 1966. (*Honolulu Star-Bulletin* photo)

lenged. Since that exchange, I was completely cut off and never had any contact with Burns or his establishment after that time. He never spoke a civil word to me again.

The basic issue of this bitter Democratic battle was succinctly stated by Dr. Walter Johnson, a nationally known political analyst, who had been close to Adlai Stevenson and was a visiting professor at the University of Hawaii in 1966. His statement was as follows:

> As a specialist in American history, I would like to point out that the primary system we adopted over 50 years ago was to give members of each political party the opportunity to select the candidate who would run in the general election.
>
> The primary was designed for one reason and that was to give the voters a choice. The present vigorous primary campaign for Lieutenant Governor here in Hawaii is to offer the Democrats that choice—the heart of the democratic process.

The statement by Walter Johnson was supported by over a hundred professors in a paid advertisement under the chairmanship of Dr. Harold Roberts and William Huntsberry. Many of them were not partisan Democrats, but the very arbitrary manner in which Governor Burns tried to impose his personal will on the entire party met with a tidal wave of resentment. The Governor never acknowledged his mistake and employed the full resources of his machine to defeat Gill. In all fairness to the Governor, it must be assumed that he was looking ahead to the next election in 1970 when his second term in office would be over. His resentment of Gill was so strong that as his successor he wanted "anybody but Gill."

Despite being outspent 2–1, we were able to swamp the opposition by more than a 2–1 margin. This might have been a Pyrrhic victory, however, as Burns decided to extend his governorship into a third term and Lieutenant Governor Gill never succeeded to the governorship.

Campaign of 1970 for Governor

The bitterness and division created by the election of 1966 carried on into the final showdown in 1970. With the momentum gained in the race for Lieutenant Governor, the Gill forces were very confident and early polls indicated a strong lead almost up to the eve of the primary election. In the final outcome, however, we lost by a surprising margin. I was campaign chairman for Gill, but from mid-June to the very end of the election, I was struck down by a severe case of tuberculosis and confined to Leahi Hospital. I was not allowed to leave even to visit my wife. Since I was completely immobilized I cannot now say too much about what developed during this bitter campaign. I would, therefore, like to defer to Tom Coffman, prize winning journalist. His book, *Catch a Wave* (University of Hawaii Press, 1973), became a classic and required reading for political science students at the University.

TV political packaging came into flower during this campaign. Costly experts and consultants were brought in to blitz the airwaves. Pre-cut television programs took over with

Paid ad by University of Hawaii professors, 1966

Governor Burns, the candidate, rarely appearing live. The packaging was so expertly done that Tom Coffman claimed it could become a model for political campaigns to come—even for those on the mainland. Grass roots and financial support were very well orchestrated under the time-tested leadership of Robert Oshiro, who has always been one of the pillars of the successful Burns organization. With Tom Coffman's permission, I quote from his book in which he wrote of a speech given by Gill on July 9, 1970 (Coffman, *Catch a Wave*, pp. 113–115).

> Gill started: The 1960s had begun with great promise, with the idealism of the civil rights movement and the national crusade against poverty. "Then it slowly turned sour under the crushing weight of Vietnam. Social programs died for lack of funds. The President (Johnson) lost credibility. The campuses fell into disorder, and the ghettos convulsed with despair."
>
> The 1960s in Hawaii had echoed the Mainland, "but in a distinctly local way. The long period of plantation colonialism was over. Our legislature, filled with bright and feisty young men, had turned out a mountain of new and innovative legislation. Finally in 1962 our party also gained the executive power, and the ability to make things happen.
>
> Growth burst out all over. Development was progress and progress was good.
>
> Some of our people became rich beyond their every expectation; most of us gained more income and more things than we ever had before. Most agreed—and still would today—that having been both poor and rich that 'rich is better.'
>
> But things began to happen to us. . . . Some of our poor and struggling public servants became less poor and struggled less. Some of the crusaders for change decided that change wasn't so important after all. The result was a slow and insidious loss of

Tom Gill For Governor Committee Is Organized, Headed By Dr. Tom Ige

Dr. Tom Ige, professor of business economics at the University of Hawaii, announced today the formation of a Gill for Governor Committee to urge Lt. Governor Thomas P. Gill to seek the Democratic nomination for governor this fall.

Dr. Ige is chairman. Attorney John H. Robinson will serve as committee treasurer. Dr. Ige also served as chairman of a similar committee during Gill's successful 1966 campaign for the office of lieutenant governor.

Dr. Ige said he has received numerous calls from people urging that Gill be a candidate for governor.

"As a result of these inquiries, we decided to form the Gill for Governor Committee."

The steering committee includes Islanders from a broad cross section of the community. Correspondence can be directed to the committee via P. O. Box 10092, Honolulu, Hawaii 96816.

The steering committee includes: Oahu — Robert Burns, Arthur Rutledge, Akito Fujikawa, Dr. Robert Clopton, Dr. Allan Saunders, Dr. John Digman, Dr. William Huntsberry, Dr. Fred Hung, August Yee, Jerry Yamaki, Dr. Allen Trubitt, Herbert Minn, G. Jovinelli, Robert Dodge, Vincent Esposito, Lydia Amona, John Fields, Dr. Duke Cho Choy, Dr. Bunkichi Uesato, Dr. George Suzuki, Dr. Grant Howard, Dr. Milton Kobayashi, Dr. Richard S. Horio, K. D. Park, Thomas Flynn, Frank Padgett, Takeo To-

TOM IGE

rigoe, Douglas Takagi, Helen Kanahele;

Hawaii: Kengo Nagasako, Cyril Kanemitsu, William J. Bonk, Richard W. Fowler, Ichiro Shikada;

Molokai: Edward Borden, Anna Goodhue;

Maui: Norman C. Franco, Bev C. Sarasin, Elmer E. Davis, Richard T. Hashi;

Kauai: Paul S. Muraoka, Tatsuo Asari, Robert Kokame;

University of Hawaii: Barbara L. Okamoto, Cynthia Yokono, Louis Chang.

Dr. Ige said his committee wants Gill to run in order to

TOM GILL

give the people of Hawaii "a meaningful choice in the primary election."

"We believe the people should choose their candidates," he said. "Tom Gill is an energetic, perceptive young man, in tune with the times. Long before 'ecology' became a popular issue, Tom Gill was pointing out what had to be done to save our environment. The same is true in the areas of housing, consumer protection, cost of living, preservation of historic sites, and many other issues now being adopted by other candidates. We need a leader."

"The overriding issue of the 1970 gubernatorial race is the economic and social direction the Hawaiian community will take in the next decade," Dr. Ige said.

"Tom Gill is uniquely qualified to serve as Hawaii's next governor. He has both the ability and the desire to cope with the hard decisions which must be made if we have any hope of preserving what is left of our islands' way of life.

"We concur in Tom Gill's belief that we can make of the 1970's what we will. The Lieutenant Governor expressed the concern of most of Hawaii's people in the statement he wrote for the Progress Edition of the Honolulu Advertiser last February. He wrote: 'If we allow the forces that have shaped our society for the last dozen years to continue undirected, our islands will lose much of their human and physical charm. Our present course is to turn Honolulu into a sordid suburb of Los Angeles and much of the neighbor islands into bellhop villages. It will destroy the natural beauty and pleasant living we prize. It will damage the roots of our self-respect and our tolerant, people-oriented society. But this need not happen. We can moderate our explosive growth build permanent and pleasant housing, prevent the paving of our open green spaces, develop transportation methods which do not destroy the earth and poison the air, and diversify our economic base for greater stability and variety of earning skills.'"

momentum. We became more interested in the form
of social innovation, not the substance.

There was talk of planning and proper land use,
but action on variances and zoning giveaways.

There was refusal to recognize the growing crises of
housing and pollution until this election was almost
upon us.

Those who sold tourism spoke of the 'golden people of Hawaii,' but turned Waikiki into an overbuilt
human bog.

Belatedly, as the smog begins to blind our view of
the mountains, some verbalize the need for pollution control, but then fail to fill necessary positions
in the control agencies and hardly move to enforce
existing laws and regulations.

There is a flutter of concern as the election
approaches, a great deal of expensive public relations, but no real answers."

Gill injected a superficially kind, but essentially cutting
word for the man of the sixties:

"I think Jack Burns is a very decent human being
and personally an honest man.

He has a deep sense of duty and loyalty to his
friends. But here lies the rub: Jack has some most
alarming friends."

At this point Gill's crowd applauded wildly.

"Too many of them are doing too well to risk the
uncertain winds of change. Even if the Governor had
no personal desire to serve a third term, I doubt very
much that his associates would allow him to retire."

The last statement proved very prophetic, as Governor
Burns passed away shortly into his third term and was succeeded by his Lieutenant Governor, George Ariyoshi. By all
accounts, the Governor was in failing health and the cam-

paign, no doubt, took a heavy toll. For me, too, this campaign was my last hurrah. This was my lowest point in politics and may have taken a great deal more out of me than I had realized.

Tom Coffman gave a detailed account of what transpired after I had to bow out of the campaign, including the entry of my wife, Fumi, into the turmoil (Coffman, *Catch a Wave* pp. 141–143).

> July ended with the resignation of Burns' deputy director of the State Department of Social Services, Royce Higa, who defected to Gill. Royce Higa, although a veteran of the famed 442nd, never had been close to Burns' inner circle, but in 1962 had campaigned for Burns in the Pearl City district, and on the strength of this and his extensive experience in public health and social work had been awarded the department position. Higa initially had been perplexed by what he regarded as lax and indecisive direction of the department. And then, having many friends in the Gill apparatus, such as Nelson Doi and Togo Nakagawa (a one-time president of the 442nd Club), he had been embarrassed and put off by Burns' 1966 campaign for Kenneth Brown. In that instance, Royce Higa had supported Gill for lieutenant governor, despite pressure from such Burns insiders as Matsuo Takabuki and Robert Oshiro. Higa was not only unmoved but disgusted when told that his role with Burns was special owing to his being the only top-level Okinawan appointee.
>
> Because a department-level appointee is expected to follow the political line of his employer, he no doubt was walking on thin ice in 1966, although Burns nonetheless had kept him on—as he had several others whose loyalty was known to lie with Tom Gill. Now in 1970, despite a last-moment attempt by Burns' administrative director, Myron Thompson, to head off the move—Myron Thompson was aware that all was not well in the depart-

Robert Oshiro. (*Honolulu Star-Bulletin* photo)

Royce Higa. (*Honolulu Star-Bulletin* photo)

ment—Higa abandoned the Burns administration in favor of Tom Gill, as Ralph Kiyosaki also had abandoned it to go with King. Higa left behind many people who regarded him as an ingrate, particularly because he had been well paid for nearly eight years. Burns himself might also have thought this but was of too magnanimous a bent to say so publicly, or for that matter allow it to be said. Privately Burns more than once had expressed bewilderment that so many people in the social development and education fields did not support him, given what he had done for these fields, particularly for education. The greatly improved University of Hawaii was a monument to John Burns' dedication to education, and yet the professors lined up with Tom Gill. Burns no doubt wondered if it was more a matter of style than substantive performance, being neither eloquent like Gill nor capable of expressing himself in a high-flown intellectual way—John Burns had dropped out after one semester and was most articulate over his breakfast table, spicing his English with well-chosen phrases in pidgin. Professors could not understand that. So on occasion there could be seen in Burns the pain of a perceived betrayal. In his own value system Burns considered loyalty—the Japanese word is *on*—to be an essential virtue. Among some of Burns' cohorts, the interpretation of this value on loyalty was narrowly political and phobic. But Burns in many instances had extended the concept beyond personal loyalties . . . Higa was a case in point. There was no other adequate explanation for his surviving in the administration after 1966, although the relationship had deteriorated, and in 1970 Higa cut the tie.

Tom Coffman continued in his account:

Royce Higa in fact was badly needed in the Gill organization, because Gill's campaign manager, Dr.

Thomas Ige of the university, had been sidelined by
an attack of tuberculosis. Higa moved in as campaign coordinator and, at peace because his political
identity finally was resolved, he enjoyed himself: He
particularly was delighted by Gills' young workers,
and they in turn regarded him as a fellow traveler on
the far side of the generational line.

Enter my wife, Fumi—Coffman continued:

Six days after Higa's resignation, Thomas Ige's
wife provided Tom Gill with yet another publicity
coup. For two and a half years Mrs. Fumi Ige had
been coordinator of the AFL-CIO's Committee on
Political Education (COPE). But on August 6, following a chaotic meeting of COPE's endorsement
committee for the Oahu division, Mrs. Ige resigned
in anger. In her resignation statement, Mrs. Ige
directed her fire on Walter Kupau, the pro-Burns
AFL-CIO president. Kupau, she claimed, had packed
the Oahu meeting in violation of the federation's
constitution to bar her from participating in the
screening of candidates. A second person boxed out
by the maneuver was Bill Abbott, the AFL-CIO executive secretary, who likewise was pro-Gill, and likewise was destined to resign. Kupau retorted that Gill
people characteristically, whenever they were out-
voted, picked up their marbles and ran—in this case,
to the press.
   But whatever the merits of the situation it probably was true that no union boss can effectually wage
public battle with an indignant woman. On leaving,
Mrs. Ige proclaimed that she no longer wanted her
name associated "with men who are bent on obtaining a COPE endorsement for Governor Burns even at
the cost of ruining the state federation." The truth
was that the fragile federation several times had
wrecked itself over politics, and was doing so again.
   Mrs. Ige subsequently set up shop in Tom Gill's

campaign headquarters downtown on King Street, just a block from Burns' headquarters, and she proceeded as chairman of a Women for Gill Committee.

On August 7, immediately following the Ige-Kupau blowup, Gill and Royce Higa huddled with fifteen AFL-CIO union bosses who had been called together by Art Rutledge. They emerged endorsing Gill for governor, adding a union blessing to Gill's candidacy beyond the highly personal attachment of Arthur Rutledge.

After all the smoke from this very bitter campaign had cleared, the bottom line was that we lost and I was never again to engage in partisan politics. I have no regrets, however, and would not have changed my course given the same circumstances. Citizenship has its duties and responsibilities.

Leahi Hospital

While being confined to Leahi Hospital for six months during the political campaign was a bitter experience, it was not all black. Under generous University sick leave provisions, I received my regular salary and was able to use the time to revise my lecture notes, which badly needed updating. As I gradually regained my health, I was expected to do some work around the hospital. I chose to trim the trees. I had watched Japanese gardeners trim and shape the trees in the public parks in Japan and admired their handiwork. They turned what would have been onerous work into artistic endeavors. I took a tree, not too tall, and studied it carefully to see what could be done. After the work was completed, I admired my handiwork as an artist would look at his painting. Tree trimming became fun.

The most benefit I derived while confined at Leahi Hospital was through a most unexpected and unusual experience. There was another patient who was at the hospital for the second time. He had a severe case of tuberculosis and required a major operation. He was over seventy years old and very

Fumiko Ige, 59, key aide to King

Fumiko Takata Ige of 3951 Lurline Drive — key aide to Lt. Gov. Jean King, former coordinator of the Hawaii State Federation of Labor's Committee on Political Action and member of the City Charter Review Commission — died Sunday at age 59.

She was born in Los Angeles. During World War II, she was interned in a Colorado relocation center for Japanese-Americans.

In 1944 she married Thomas Ige in Minneapolis, where he was attending the University of Minnesota and teaching economics. The Iges came to to Hawaii when he joined the

Mrs. Ige

faculty of the University of Hawaii in 1953.

In 1959, Mrs. Ige co-chaired the Hawaii Table Grape Boycott Committee, which backed striking field workers in California.

Besides her husband, Mrs. Ige leaves a son, Glenn; a daughter, Dianne; her mother, Sei Takata of Los Angeles; and a sister, Mrs. Fred I. (Ruth) Kosaka of Los Angeles.

Friends may call 7 to 8 p.m. tomorrow at Makiki Christian Church, with services over the ashes scheduled at 8 p.m. The family requests casual attire.

Editorial *Honolulu Advertiser* May 15, 1979

depressed, seldom socializing with other patients. His name was Kamado Miyasato. For many years he had worked on a sugar plantation in Kohala on the island of Hawaii. As I got to know him, I discovered he had been a serious student of the Okinawan *samisen* (a three stringed musical instrument) and I asked him to give me some lessons. Since there were no such instruments at the hospital and he had none at home, I asked my wife to bring me two *samisens* from my dad's collection. My dad had dabbled in the art for some time with his teacher, Mr. Izumigawa.

This turned out to be quite a break for both of us. We would quietly retire into the recesses of the shower rooms during off-hours to practice for hours everyday. Miyasato was most meticulous and stuck closely to the music sheets. He even taught me the correct pronunciation of the different Okinawan phrases, as well as the delicate nuances of Okinawan music. The first piece he taught me was the best. It was the *Nu bui Udichi*, a semi-classical song from the days when Okinawa was still an independent kingdom but had to pay tribute to the shogunate in Kyoto. It tells of the long yearly journey on the famous Tokaido Road. It is a very beautiful song with that certain sadness that seems to characterize Okinawan music. I still think of my old teacher, Miyasato, when I play this song. During the four months I was under the tutelage of this fine teacher, I mastered about five other songs and in the process learned a great deal about Okinawan history and culture. At long last I came to appreciate Okinawan music, which to me until then was only somewhat haunting and intriguing.

Although my political involvement ended with the 1970 gubernatorial race of 1970, my wife, Fumi, continued with the campaign of Jean King for the Lieutenant Governorship in 1978. Again, the basic fight was the liberal elements of the Democratic Party fighting the establishment. Fortunately, Jean King prevailed against all odds, but the campaign took a very heavy toll on my wife. After serving as King's office manager, she died on the job from what was officially known as "stress." She lived her life always fighting for the underdog and I'm sure she had no regrets.

CHAPTER 12

Retirement Years

In his farewell address before the joint session of Congress, retiring General Douglas MacArthur stated majestically, "Old soldiers never die, they just fade away." I have been in the process of fading away prior to my retirement from the University in 1980 at the age of sixty-three.

My justification for including this last chapter is twofold: Thousands of my generation are also going into their twilight years in Hawaii, and they face the same problems and experiences I face. I certainly do not view myself as a kind of model senior citizen, but I see myself more as a point of reference from which others may derive some benefit. Secondly, reflecting back on the experiences of my long journey, I wish to update some of my observations which, in some cases, were made more than fifty years ago. One enters the twilight years with whatever he has brought with him from his younger, more productive years. Nostalgia is, in a real sense, a mild affliction among the aging, and I'll try to minimize this for I am fully aware that the younger generation hearing about the old days gets bored and impatient.

Health

The first point of consideration is certainly health. I see some of my compatriots in their late seventies or early eighties still able to walk and play eighteen holes of golf at the Ala Wai public course. I marvel and envy them as I myself cannot walk even nine holes. In health matters, I would have to say I have been on the less fortunate side. I have spent more time in hospitals than all my brothers and sister combined. Besides my wartime disabilities and a bout with tuberculosis, I have had surgery for Bell's Palsy, defined as "a suddenly occurring unilateral facial paralysis of unknown etiology." Whenever I smile now, my face turns into a slightly cynical-looking twist on the left side. A far more serious disability for me is arthritis. I have had to replace both of my hip joints (total prosthesis). Whenever I pass through the metal detection booth at the airport, an alarm is set off by my steel hips. With these artificial hips, it became painful for me to pick up a golf ball on the green. In other aspects of health, I consider myself fortunate. My heart has always been strong and my blood pressure is relatively low.

The more important point here is what to do to maintain one's health. Besides regular checkups with my doctor at the Honolulu Medical Group, my chief recourse has been The SPA Health & Fitness Centers. I usually use the one at the corner of Beretania and Punahou. To me, this is the best bargain in town. I paid $300 about seven years ago for a lifetime membership and I have been able to utilize their manifold facilities on Tuesdays, Thursdays, and Saturdays ever since. Skipping all the muscle-building apparatus on the main floor, I go to the basement where I can relax and exercise in the swimming pool. A large and turbulent jacuzzi is especially suited for my ailing legs. The swimming pool is fifty feet long and I try to swim underwater the entire length of the pool to strengthen my lungs. The sauna and steam baths are most helpful in relaxing and in maintaining my weight. I enjoy the facilities every week and every month without additional cost. I can't imagine a better bargain!

Finances

One generally expects a professional economist to have accumulated a tidy little fortune before retirement but I must admit, almost apologetically, that such was not the case with me. The only real asset I had was my fee-simple house on

Home on Maunalani Heights, 1960

Maunalani Heights. I bought the 12,000 square foot lot in 1958 at a cost of 90 cents a square foot and had the house built the following year. I added a full-basement recreation room with an outdoor swimming pool. I must say that the view from this 800-foot level was truly panoramic with Diamond Head, Waikiki, and the wide expanse of the blue Pacific below. Upon retirement, I decided to sell this house. My wife had passed away the year before; both my children had left home; and it seemed foolish for me to continue living in the big three-bedroom house all by myself. With the gain I derived from the sale, I was able to pay for a luxury condominium a block below Roosevelt High School on Mott-Smith Drive. No more yard work for me!

For the retired, income is in some ways more important than assets. In this regard, mine has been modest but adequate. The Hawaii State retirement system, social security, and military disability provide regular income for me. With hardly any fixed liability, I am able to make ends meet with enough left over for an occasional pleasure trip.

Family

I have two children. My daughter, Dianne, after graduating from my old alma mater, the University of Wisconsin, has gradually worked herself up in the highly competitive clothing industry in New York City. As a buyer for the Associated Merchandising Corp., she traveled regularly to Paris, France; Florence, Italy; Tokyo; Seoul; Taiwan; and Hong Kong until she became a divisional vice president with less time to travel. My son, Glenn, after serving in the Medical Corp of the U.S. Navy in Vietnam, came back to work as a paramedic in Honolulu. He and his family live about a half mile from our condominium in Makiki. In 1981 I remarried. My second wife, Hiroko, was born in Kyoto, Japan. She is fluent in Japanese but limited in English. She has been attending special English classes for the last four years. She has recently become addicted to golf and plays more often than I do, walking instead of riding.

Television

The bane and addiction of many a senior citizen may be the "tube." I must confess, this has been a serious problem with me, at least my wife thinks so. Upon retirement, I splurged on two things, a small Cadillac and the biggest and most expensive television set I could find. I anticipated that I would be spending many hours before the "tube," so I got the best. This addiction would not have been so demanding except that since my retirement, there has been a sudden explosion of sports on television. I have always been a sports fan but the weekly menu of sporting events provided now is something like looking at the menu of a fancy Chinese restaurant. One weekend last fall in football Notre Dame was playing Michigan, Southern California played Stanford, U.C.L.A. was at Nebraska, Hawaii was opposing Colorado (delayed), and the semifinals of the U.S. Open tennis tournament were also being televised. How can paradise surpass this! I enjoy the

My wife, Hiroko, 1982

Son, Glenn, and my grandson, Jonathan, 1985

Family photo, 1987. *Left to right:* Marylyn and Glenn, Tom, Dianne and Dave Witt

Last family photo of my brothers and sister, 1988. *Left to right, back row:* Tom, Hiroshi, Kosaburo. *Front row:* Yasuichi, Yoshiko

play-offs in both baseball and later football and by delayed tel-
ecast, I rarely miss sumo tournaments televised from Japan.
The non-sports programs also have much to offer. I find live
televising of important congressional hearings and sessions
on C-SPAN II especially rewarding. I don't think we oldsters
need to apologize for our addiction to television, as we do not
have work schedules to worry about. To me, this is an integral
part of enjoying my retirement.

Golf

Bill Kwan of the *Honolulu Star-Bulletin* recently wrote in his
entertaining column that golf is the game particularly suited
for the elderly and even the slightly infirm. I cannot agree
with him more. It helps me to get away from home and television into the sunshine and the green expanse accessible all
year around in Hawaii. Not only is the physical exercise bene-
ficial, but the mental relaxation is even more rewarding. The
social aspects of golf should not be underestimated either.
Playing in a foursome you really get to know and make new
friends. On the golf course, there is hardly any distinction
between rich or poor, between races, between young and old,
between men or women. With proper handicapping, almost
anyone can play in a foursome and enjoy the game.

I currently belong to two golf clubs. The Bob Tanaka Inc.
group plays every Wednesday at the various courses on Oahu,
with occasional forays to the neighbor islands and even to the
mainland and Canada. I am especially appreciative of the tol-
erance club members display when playing with a disabled
golfer with a 26 handicap. The socializing during and after the
games is also enjoyable.

The Kin Golf Club plays only one Sunday a month. It has a
strong ethnic flavor—not only Okinawan but also a more narrow appeal to descendants of the Kin Village in Okinawa.
Many of my relatives participate, including my wife. In a
sense, the club tries to perpetuate ethnic identity and to pro-
mote greater familiarity among the group. Club tournaments
are conducted very creditably by the Nakama family headed

by Larry and his brothers, Bob and Sueo, and their wives. As young kids we grew up together on the rice farms in Kahaluu Valley. Larry's son, Lloyd, is the pro at the Olomana Golf Links and Sueo's son, Casey, is a touring pro and one of the top golfers in Hawaii.

My most memorable and rewarding golfing experience came in the summer of 1979, just before retirement. The former president of the University, Dr. Fujio Matsuda, sponsored the all-university golf tournament at the Kunia golf course, which drew about 200 golfers. I rode in the same car with Jack Nagoshi, a former director of the Youth Development Research Center at the University. I shot a net 58 with an 18 handicap. Jack, as a 7 handicapper, shot much better than I did, but because of his low handicap did not win the overall prize. My triumph was given prominent coverage by the press and I must say I was more embarrassed than proud. I was, however, happy to say goodbye to the University in this manner.

The University

For the second generation of the immigrants who came to Hawaii to labor in the cane and pineapple fields of Hawaii, the University of Hawaii was more than just an institution of higher learning. It was a major path of advancement to the higher rungs of society and was regarded reverently by the older as well as the younger generation. Almost my entire life revolved around the University and to it I owe whatever success I have had in life. From a third-rate school of 2,000 students in 1936, it has emerged into a huge conglomerate with campuses and programs spread throughout the state. I cannot help but marvel at the superb job done by Dr. Fujio Matsuda, Dr. Albert Simone, and others in upgrading the quality of the multi-faceted programs, as well as the faculty.

Take the athletic program at the University as an example. Though athletics is by no means the most important aspect of the University's activities, the high visibility of the athletic program provides good insight to what has been transpiring on the main Manoa campus. In the mid-sixties the famous "Crazy Legs" Hirsh was invited to evaluate the intercollegiate facilities at our University. He was at that time an executive of the professional Los Angeles Rams football team. He had had a brilliant playing career in college and in professional football and later became athletic director at the University of Wisconsin. His report was highly critical, to put it mildly, and made University and state officials aware of the dire need to upgrade our athletic program and facilities.

The new athletic complex in what we used to refer to as the "old quarry site" is truly astounding. What may be lacking are a big basketball field house and a football stadium on the University of Hawaii campus, but the availability of the Neal S. Blaisdell Center for basketball and the Aloha Stadium for football make these shortfalls somewhat irrelevant. The crown jewel on the lower campus of the University now, of course, is the magnificent baseball stadium, generally regarded as the best on any university campus throughout the country. Baseball coach Les Murakami can now be proud to invite any team to play here. I shake my head when I recall the makeshift diamond we had in the mid-fifties, hardly fit for even scrimmage games.

The emergence of national stature teams in baseball, football, and volleyball for both men and women, have captured the attention and enthusiasm throughout the state. I feel good listening to people talking now about "our" team at the University.

Okinawa

I last revisited Okinawa in the fall of 1985 on a golfing safari with the Nakama brothers. I recall the wartime destruction and demoralization and was greatly impressed and encouraged with the tremendous strides made in recent years in all aspects of life in Okinawa. Until recently, I believed this prefecture was on the bottom rung of all the prefectures in Japan. Recent surveys placed it in about the middle or slightly higher in the standings of Japanese prefectures. I was particularly taken with the development of super highways stretching the entire length of the long main island of Okinawa all the way up to Motobu, where a world oceanic exposition was held in the late seventies.

An amusing incident occurred during this visit which struck me as outlandish but indicative of the heights some have attained. Bob Nakama and I were having a cup of coffee in Naha with a native he had come to know while working there briefly in the post-war years. During the course of our conversation this native, Yoshio Akamine, stated that he knew of a place where they served the best Okinawan *soba* (noodles). We were delighted to accept his invitation to take us there. To our surprise, he drove us to the Naha Airport. From there he taxied out his private plane and flew us to Kume Jima, some hundred miles to the west of the main island. The *soba* there was indeed superb, but such conspicuous display of extravagance overwhelmed me. This, of course, was not typical of even the high life in modern-day Okinawa but it forced me to rethink my image of war-torn Okinawa.

A few days later I made it a special point to revisit the battle sites in the Kerama Retto, some twenty-five miles southwest of Naha. Catching an interisland ferry, we leisurely circled the islands of Aka, Zamami, and Tokashiki. It was a very emotional sojourn for me as I nostalgically recalled the bittersweet days fighting the remnants of the Japanese troops in the hills and valleys of these beautiful islands. Even on these remote islands one can easily see the signs of what we may loosely call progress. There was not a single automobile on Aka Jima during the war; only dirt roads encircled parts of the island. Now I saw a new waterfront with concrete wharves with many fishing boats secured and trucks loading and unloading cargo. On Zamami the transformation was even more startling. Even during the war I had thought that the sand beaches there were the best I had ever seen, far superior to Waikiki. These beaches have now been discovered by the tourist trade and the place is being rapidly made into a tourist destination. I saw some young people windsurfing offshore and somehow I felt sad that this piece of "God's little acre" will soon become another sacrifice to the altar of the seekers of the sun and fun. I did not bother to land on Tokashiki Island, as my memory of the pain and suffering there would have been too much.

Kahaluu Valley

Having started the account of my long journey in Kahaluu Valley, I conclude with a nostalgic visit to my old hometown. It may suffice merely to say that I was a stranger in my own hometown, as so many others have been in other places. Paved roads crisscrossed the valley, some with concrete sidewalks and overhead lighting. Where no haoles lived in the valley when I grew up there, today there are more haoles than Okinawans. Somehow one can hardly recapture the feel of the old days, but, here and there, the ghosts from the past rekindle the bittersweet memories of days long gone and forgotten. Above all else, I cannot, and will not, forget the hardships our parents endured in their struggle to make it possible for their children to enjoy a better life in the future.

As important as are the physical changes in Kahaluu are the psychological changes that have transpired among those of us descendants of Okinawan immigrants. While growing up in the valley we definitely suffered from inferiority complexes that were strong and all pervasive. To be pointed out as an Okinawan hurt us deeply and our heritage and culture were sources of embarrassment.

With the unceasing efforts of various organizations to enhance and perpetuate our culture, this cultural handicap has largely disappeared and a new feeling of pride is beginning to emerge in many of us. The present effort by the United Okinawan Association to establish the Bunka-Kai-Kan Cultural Center will be a culmination of this almost century-long struggle for recognition and respect in the multi-ethnic society of Hawaii—*Chibariyo.*